GROWING IN JOY

GOD'S WAY TO INCREASE JOY IN ALL OF LIFE

RON KLUG

AUGSBURG Publishing House • Minneapolis

GROWING IN JOY

Library of Congress Catalog Card No. 82-072637

International Standard Book No. 0-8066-1943-0

Photos: Bob Taylor, 11, 111; Camerique, 18; Paul Conklin, 28; Florence Sharp, 42; Vernon Sigl, 63; Paul Schrock, 89, 98.

Manufactured in the United States of America

To Catharine and Ceil,
Pat and Rod,
helpers of my joy

Contents

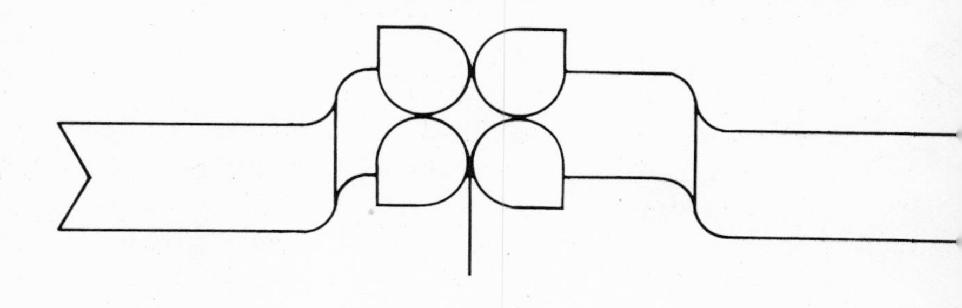

About This Book

Are you filled with the joy of the Lord? Is your life overflowing with joy? If so, you probably don't need this book. In fact, I wish you would write one for me!

If you believe there is in the Christian life a greater potential for joy than you are now experiencing, this book may help you.

It grew out of my own questions about joy and my own search for greater joy. What really is joy? I wondered. How do we get it? How can we have more of it? How can it be sustained in the midst of difficulties and troubles?

I began by studying what the Bible says about *joy*—and related words like *rejoice* and *joyful*. You will find most of these key statements from God's Word quoted in this book.

I then went on to read a variety of Christian writers to learn what they had discovered about joy. I was especially interested in the experiences of those who had found joy in suffering and persecution. You will read some of their words here too.

I also reflected on my own experience and that of friends and acquaintances. Who are the joyful people? What is the secret of their joy?

I have put what I learned into 31 chapters, each based on one scripture passage which speaks of joy. You may first want to read the book straight through to see what it says. But then I hope you will read it a chapter a day for a month. I say this because I believe we experience the joy of which the Bible speaks as we saturate our minds with the truths about joy, as we ponder them and let the Holy Spirit renew our minds. For it is the Holy Spirit working through his Word who brings us joy.

At the end of each chapter is an affirmation, a short personalized statement of a particular truth about joy. Let it be the key thought you take from your reading. Repeat it to yourself often during the day and before you sleep and when you awaken. Then this truth will seep into your soul where it will produce joy in your life.

As I studied the subject of joy, I began to see how wide a concept it is; it touches every phase of Christian life and teaching. I found no simple definition of joy, no simple formula for achieving instant joy. Rather, I believe that as we study what the Bible says about joy, first from one angle, then another, and another, and as we apply these truths to our lives, our joy will increase.

In Jesus' parable of the talents, the returning master commends each faithful servant with the words, "Well done. Come enter into the joy of the Lord." As you ponder these great Bible truths about joy, I pray that you too, like many other Christians, may "enter into the joy of the Lord."

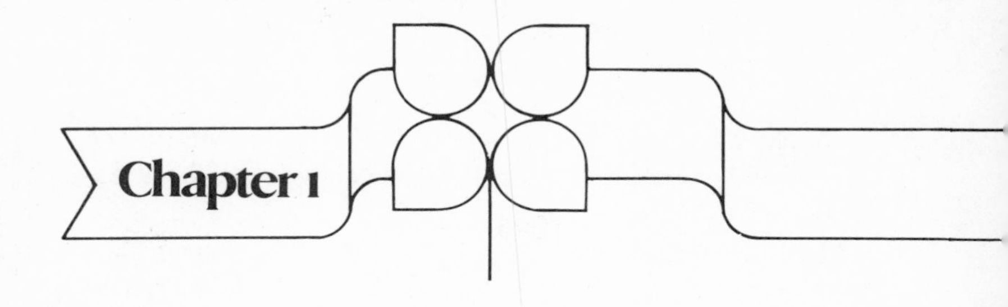

The Fullness of Joy

These things I have spoken to you, that my joy may be in you, and that your joy may be full.

John 15:11

The basis for our exploration into joy is this conviction: God wants us to be full of joy; joy is God's will for us. Jesus said, "These things I have spoken to you, that my joy may be in you, and that your joy may be full."

Ask yourself, "Do I really believe that God's intention for me is a joy-filled life?"

Maybe that seems obvious to you, but there are those who deny it. There are those who see the Christian life as a dreary, serious, grim business. There are others who think that our goal should be to feel as miserable as possible, that we should wallow in feelings of guilt, helplessness, and despair, and that then God is especially pleased with us. Some claim that any talk about joy is "emotionalism," which they see as inferior to a purely "intellectual" Christianity. All these people would claim that it is somehow wrong to desire joy. Yet Jesus said his desire is "that your joy may be full." And David prayed,

"Fill me with joy and gladness" (Ps. 51:8). So we can be clear on this point: it is all right to want joy in our lives, for that is what God wants too.

Martin Luther agreed with this idea. He said, "God wants us to be cheerful, and he hates sadness. For had he wanted us to be sad, he would not have given us the sun, the moon, and the various fruits of the earth. All this he gave us for our good cheer."

I believe that this desire for joy is built into us, that it is one of the ways God calls us to himself. Nearly everyone is searching for joy, but not all are looking in the right place. Some seek it in material possessions, or in entertainment, or in immorality, liquor, or drugs, or in a desperate bid for success and popularity. In other words, they look for joy in almost every place except where it can be found—in God himself.

C. S. Lewis wrote, "God has designed the human machine to run on Himself. He Himself is the fuel our spirits were designed to burn, or the food our spirits were designed to feed on. There is no other. That is why it is just no good asking God to make us happy without bothering about religion. God cannot give us happiness and peace apart from Himself, because it is not there. There is no such thing."

This does not mean that people who do not know God in Christ are totally unhappy. We have only to look around to see that this is not true. Yet in God we can find a level of joy that goes beyond a shallow or fragile happiness which has never faced up to the reality of sin or the heartbreak of the world. We are made for more than that. We are here to develop personalities capable of communion with God and to pass on the good news of God's love.

Jesus said, "These things I have spoken to you, that my joy may be *in you.*" Christian joy is not something that comes

to us from the outside, something that must be added to our life from beyond us. Rather it wells up from deep within us, from the depths of our being, where God himself dwells. For the words Paul wrote about himself apply to every Christian, "It is no longer I who live, but Christ who lives in me" (Gal. 2:20). And as Christ lives in us, as we live in relationship with him, his joy is expressed in us and through us.

You may be thinking, "I know Christ. I believe he is my Savior, but I am not experiencing much joy in my life. What's wrong?"

In *Fruits of the Spirit* Charles R. Hembree wrote: "Joy is like a well containing sweet water. It is not enough to know that water is there or even to drill the well. If the well is to be useful, the water must be brought to the surface. Those who know Christ have found the source of joy, but some have not drawn from the well, and, therefore, their joy remains buried."

The purpose of this book is to help us learn to draw from the well, to bring the water to the surface, to discover how the joy which God wants us to have can be released in our lives.

I am filled with the joy of Christ.

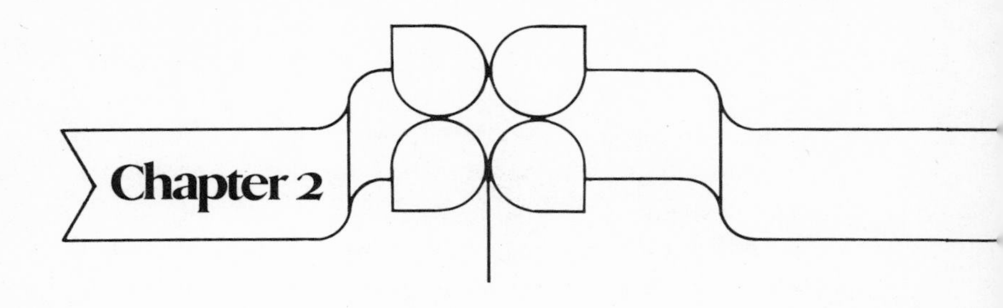

The Joy of Repentance

There will be more joy in heaven over one sinner who repents.
Luke 15:7

The search for joy begins with the putting away of sin. The first step in entering into God's joy is repentance. The apostle James writes: "Cleanse your hands, you sinners, and purify your hearts, you men of double mind. Be wretched and mourn and weep. Let your laughter be turned to mourning and your joy to dejection. Humble yourselves before the Lord and he will exalt you" (James 4:8-10).

We can begin our quest for joy by taking an honest look at our lives—our deeds, our words, our thoughts—to see where we fall short of the life God intends for us. We often have a clear idea of God's will for us; we have the words of Scripture and the example of Jesus before us, showing us what we can be. And we can ask God to show us the aspects of our lives that are contrary to his commands, all those things that are also the enemies of our joy.

The well-known Chinese Christian, Watchman Nee, said, "If you have no rest or joy, you must be holding onto something which you are unwilling to give up . . . if you are really willing to take up the Lord's yoke and learn of Him, you will be filled with joy and praise."

This self-examination may be a painful process, yet in another sense it can be a great relief. For it means we don't have to pretend that we're perfect, not even to ourselves. Self-justification always stifles the joy of repentance. When we honestly admit our faults, we can say like the prodigal son, "I will arise and go to my father, and I will say to him, 'Father, I have sinned. . . .' " (Matt. 15:18). And the waiting Father will lift us up and fill us with joy.

Repentance is not just admitting our faults, not just a negative process. Repentance is changing our way of looking at life. It is a new, positive change of direction which affects all of life—the use of our time, our money, our abilities, the way we relate to others. It is a kind of homecoming and therefore is accompanied by joy, a joy shared by the angels in heaven (Luke 15:10).

James writes, "Cleanse your hands, you sinners, and purify your hearts, you men of double mind." The first, "Cleanse your hands," suggests that we look at our deeds, at those acts which displease God and interfere with our joy—the cutting remarks we make about others, our impatience with our families, the petty dishonesties, the selfish use of time and money—all the actions for which we need to ask forgiveness and which we need to bring under the control of God's Spirit.

The apostle's second command, "Purify your hearts, you men of double mind," directs us to look at our thoughts, our habitual ways of thinking. What are the words we say to ourselves each moment as we go about the business of our day? If we can become more aware of our habitual thoughts, we can go a long way toward identifying—and overcoming—the enemies of our joy. Minds which are filled with anxiety, worry, jealousy, faultfinding, resentment, and self-pity have little room for the joy of the Lord. R. W. Dale says, "We ask God to forgive us for our evil thoughts and evil temper, but rarely, if ever, ask him to forgive us for our sadness." Yet that very sadness is often a sign that we are out of harmony with God and his will for us. We may find this disciplining of our thoughts to be much harder than changing some outward actions, yet it is just here that the battle may need to be fought.

This repentance for our thoughts and deeds is not just a one-time act; it is a daily need. Each day we need to examine ourselves to see where our thoughts and words and deeds are out of line with God's will, and each day we need to ask his forgiveness. This need not be a miserable recitation of failure, muttered in abject fear. Those of us who are parents know that we are happy when a child says, simply, "I'm sorry."

Mother Basilea Schlink, in her book *Repentance—the Joy-Filled Life,* writes: "The first characteristic of the kingdom of Heaven—joy, great joy—will be kindled through contrition and repentance. Repentance is the only gate through which the Gospel is received. Repentance is the entrance to the joy-filled life with Christ. It is the prerequisite for attaining forgiveness, and wherever forgiveness is received there is salvation and joy."

I find joy in repentance.

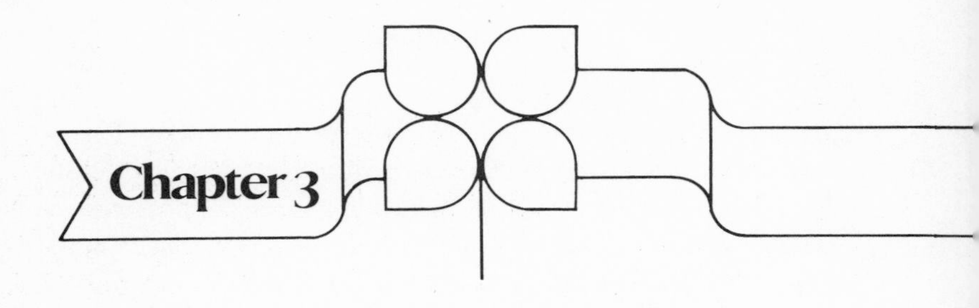

The Joy of Salvation

With joy you will draw water from the wells of salvation.
Isaiah 12:3

We have seen that God wants us to be joyful; his will for us is joy. And we have seen that the way to joy begins with repentance—taking an honest look at our thoughts, our words, our deeds, identifying that which blocks the free flow of God's joy in us. Our next step is to look at the provision God has made for our lives.

As I was studying the Bible verses dealing with joy, I was brought up short by Psalm 51:8: "Fill me with joy and gladness; let the bones which thou hast broken rejoice." I could understand the first part; everyone I know wants to be filled with joy and gladness. But what about that second part: does that mean that *God* breaks my bones? In what sense is that true?

I believe that sometimes God has to let us get to the end of our rope. He lets us pursue our own way until we come to the end of our resources and have to admit our own emptiness and brokenness. We reach a deadend, broken by our own rebellion and willfulness, broken against God's laws, against the moral order of the universe. Yet even this is God's mercy, even this shows his love, for he does not let us go our own way forever, but he brings us to the place of brokenness and despair so that we cry out to him for salvation, for healing, for restoration and renewal. And then he is there, the waiting Father.

Billy Graham has said, "In God's economy you must go down into the valley of grief before you can scale the heights of spiritual glory. You must become tired and weary of living alone before you seek and find the fellowship of Christ. You must come to the end of self before you really begin to live. The mourning of inadequacy is a weeping that catches the attention of God. . . . The happiest day of my life was when I realized that my own ability, my own goodness, and my own morality was insufficient in the sight of God; and I publicly and openly acknowledged my need of Christ. I am not exaggerating when I say that my mourning was turned into joy, and my sighing to singing."

The prophet Jeremiah gives a vivid picture of the search for life apart from God: "My people have committed two evils: they have forsaken me, the fountain of living waters, and hewed out cisterns for themselves, broken cisterns, that can hold no water" (Jer. 2:13). By contrast, Isaiah shows the opposite action, the turning to God: "With joy you will draw water from the wells of salvation."

One day when Jesus was thirsty after a morning of traveling, he stopped at a well where he met a woman of doubtful reputation. After asking her for a drink, Jesus said to her, "If you knew the gift of God, and who it is that is saying to you, 'Give me a drink,' you would have asked him, and he would have given you living water."

Misunderstanding him, the woman said, "Sir, you have

nothing to draw with, and the well is deep; where do you get that living water?"

Jesus answered, "Everyone who drinks of this water that I shall give him will never thirst; the water that I shall give him will become in him a spring of water welling up to eternal life" (John 4:10-14).

This water that Jesus gives can be summed up in one word: *salvation. Salvation* is a rich word. It includes forgiveness of sins and life with God beyond death, but it also means wholeness, restored relationships, health of body and mind. All the good things God has for us are gathered up in that word *salvation.*

All the blessings of salvation come to us when we stop trusting in our own strength and wisdom and goodness and turn to God as we learn to know him in Jesus Christ. Eric Malte says in *New Joy for Daily Living,* "Only in fellowship and union with Jesus Christ—only by trusting in His person and saving work, not in anything that man might add or contribute—are true and lasting joy to be found."

David writes in Psalm 51: "Restore to me the joy of thy salvation." He thereby indicates that the joy of salvation can be lost. We restore an object that once was good but now is tarnished or ruined. We may once have experienced a flush of joy when we first became a Christian or at some peak experience in our Christian life. That joy can be restored as we look away from ourselves and to God who promises us salvation. As we continue to turn to him in every need, we will draw water from the wells of salvation, and God will fill us with joy and gladness.

With joy will I draw water from the wells of salvation.

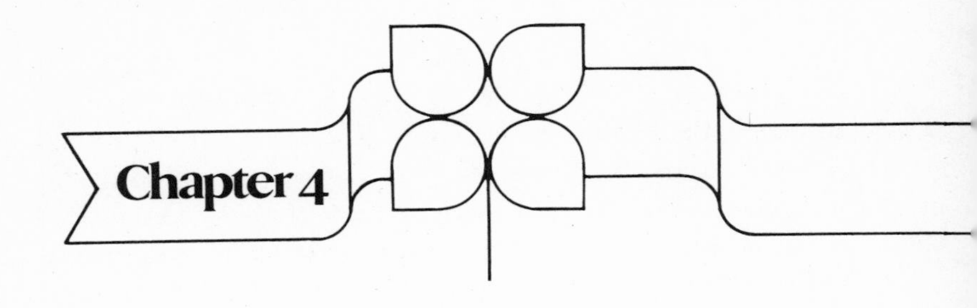

Joy, the Fruit of the Holy Spirit

The fruit of the Spirit is love, joy, peace, patience, kindness, goodness, faithfulness, gentleness, self-control.

Galatians 5:22-23

Nowhere in the Bible is the beauty of Christian life described more succinctly than in Paul's wonderful list of the fruits of the Spirit: love, joy, peace, patience, kindness, goodness, faithfulness, gentleness, self-control—all traits we admire in others and desire in ourselves.

Joy takes a prominent place as one of these nine fruits of the Spirit. To me this suggests two important truths.

First of all, if joy is the fruit of the Holy Spirit, then you can't have one without the other. If you want the joy, then you have to want the Holy Spirit too. And that means your whole life must be yielded to the Spirit's direction. It doesn't work to want the joy of the Holy Spirit without being willing to let him have control over your life.

To put it another way: joy is *one* of the fruits of the Spirit, one of the beautiful traits of character which the Spirit wishes to produce in us. But there are eight other traits which the Spirit is just as eager to produce in us: love, peace, patience, kindness, goodness, faithfulness, gentleness, and self-control. We can and should desire them all. It is not for us to pick and choose among them. It won't do to say, "Yes, I'd like joy in my life, but I don't want patience. I want to go on exercising my right to fly off the handle whenever I please." We can't say, "Yes, I want joy, but I don't want self-control. I want the right to do whatever I feel like doing at any given moment." We can't say, "I want more joy in my life, but not more kindness. I want to go on being as selfish as I've always been." When we let him, the Holy Spirit develops all these fruits in us. If we choose to resist him in one area, we block him in all.

This means that all acts, thoughts, and tendencies which oppose the pressure of the Holy Spirit must be eliminated. Evelyn Underhill says in her book *Fruits of the Spirit:* "This will include all that diminishes or opposes joy and peace which ought to spread from Christian souls; all deliberate restlessness, fuss, anxiety, all suspiciousness and bitterness. . . . All these are sins against the Spirit of Joy and Peace. If we want to be sturdy Christians, strong in spirit, useful to God, all these have got to go."

Secondly, if joy is a fruit of the Holy Spirit, it is not something we have to produce by our own willpower. It is the Spirit who produces this fruit in us.

I remember a young girl I met at a writers conference. She told us that because she was a Christian, she was perfectly joyful all the time. But it was easy to see that she had to exert great effort to maintain this "joy" in the presence of others. And once, when she thought no one was looking, I saw the mask slip, and the despair and self-doubt that were lurking underneath were all too evident. This self-produced elation is not the joy which is the fruit of the Holy Spirit.

Joy is not something we have to produce by our own power. In fact, if we try, the law of reverse effect takes over; the harder you try to be joyful, the more impossible it becomes.

Here is one of the places where the old slogan makes sense: Let go and let God. We have to let go of our own efforts to produce joy and let God produce joy in us. We also have to let go of all the false methods we have for seeking joy: alcohol, drugs, wealth, sinful pleasures. If we look for joy in these, we are not looking for it as a fruit of the Spirit. We have to let go of these false hopes, ignore their false promises, and let God give us his joy.

If joy is the fruit of the Spirit in us, then what is there for us to do? The answer to that lies in Jesus' words in John 15: "I am the vine, you are the branches. He who abides in me, and I in him, he it is that bears much fruit" (v. 5). Here Jesus gives a direct command, "Abide in me." We abide in Jesus as we trust him, as we allow his words to abide in us, as we look to him in prayer. If we do that, we are fulfilling the condition for fruit-bearing. As we do that, the life-giving Spirit flows through us, and we will bear much fruit, including the fruit of joy.

Good farmers, no matter how ambitious or hardworking, have to await the time of maturity for their crops. We too may have to await the time of maturity in our Christian lives. We may become impatient and want the fruit to appear faster or in greater abundance, but that leads only to frustration. Our need is to abide in Jesus, to pray for fruit, to expect it in faith, and to wait for the Holy Spirit to produce in us his joy and all his other fruits—in his good time.

Joy is the fruit of the Holy Spirit.

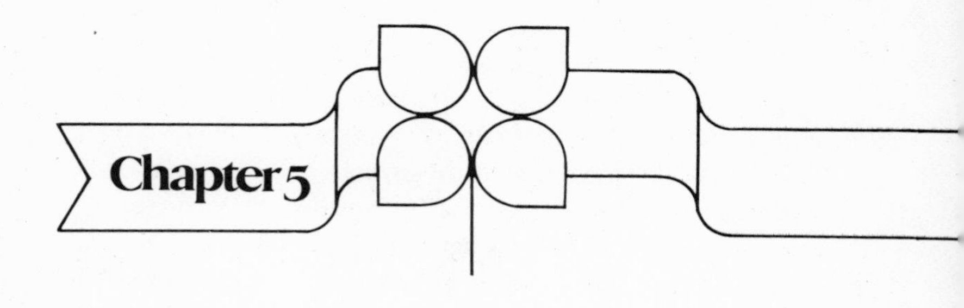

Joy of the Kingdom

For the kingdom of God is not food and drink but righteousness and peace and joy in the Holy Spirit; he who thus serves Christ is acceptable to God and approved by men.
Romans 14:17-18

As Christians we have been made members of God's kingdom. God is our ruler; we are his subjects. His will becomes our will as we choose his way of life rather than our own. Oswald Chambers said, "The joy that Jesus gives is the result of our disposition being at one with his own disposition."

To live in God's kingdom is to live under his rule. As we submit our will to his will, we will find "righteousness and peace and joy in the Holy Spirit." Insofar as our will is in harmony with God's will, we will know the joy of Christian living. Evelyn Underhill wrote, "This is the secret of joy. We shall no longer strive for our own way; but commit ourselves, easily and simply, to God's way, acquiesce in his will and in so doing find our peace."

We do this by making a beginning, by an act of will, saying, "Lord, I give myself completely into your hands. I want to will only what you want. My whole life belongs to you." Then as time goes on, God will probably show us areas of our lives which are not in harmony with his will. This surrendering to God is not a one-time act, but a continuing process.

Such self-examination may be painful; such obedience may be costly. This is the opposite of the "cheap grace" which is content with forgiveness of sins while evading full commitment to God's will. Yet it is only this commitment, made to the full extent that we are able at any given moment, that is pleasing to God. And the ancient writer of Ecclesiastes said, "To the man who pleases him God gives wisdom and knowledge and joy" (2:26).

This harmony with the will of God can take two forms. One is obedience to the commands of God, attention to the tasks he clearly places before us. Mark Twain once said that he was not troubled by the parts of the Bible he could not understand, but by the parts he *did* understand. Our problem is not usually that we fail to understand what we are to do. My experience is that I usually know full well what God wants me to do this day or this hour or this minute. My problem is that I don't *feel* like doing it, so I find some way to pursue my own will rather than his.

When I'm tempted in this way, I try to remember the words of George Macdonald, the writer who meant so much to C. S. Lewis: "Troubled soul, thou art not bound to feel but thou art bound to arise. God loves thee whether thou feelest or not. Thou canst not love when thou wilt, but thou art bound to fight the hatred in thee to the last. Try not to feel good when thou art not good, but cry to Him who is good. He changes not because thou changest. Nay, He has an especial tenderness of love towards thee for that thou art in the dark and hast no light, and His heart is glad when thou dost arise and say, 'I will go to my Father.' . . . Fold the arms of thy faith, and wait in the quietness until light goes up in thy darkness. Fold the arms of thy faith I say, but not of thy action: bethink thee of something that thou oughtest to do, and go to do it, if it be but the sweeping of a room, or the preparing of a meal, or a visit to a friend. Heed not thy feelings: Do thy work."

Harmony with the will of God takes a second form: submitting to the will of God in matters where we have no choice. Situations come into our lives over which we have no control, situations that may be threatening, saddening, even terrifying. If we chafe under them, rebel against them, fight against them, the pain only increases. If we can learn to accept them as coming through the hands of a loving Father and by his permission, then we can submit to them, decrease their power to hurt us, and even find joy in the struggle. A mother in childbirth knows that struggling against the contractions of labor only intensifies the pain and fear. If she can learn to relax and submit, the discomfort is still there, but it is manageable.

The Chinese Christian leader Watchman Nee said, "If we wish to be a useful and valuable vessel before God, we should not murmur but instead be joyful and restful towards all the things that He permits to come upon us. Let us say to God: 'O Father, I thank You, for all that You have permitted to come upon me is good.' By submitting ourselves to the will of God our hearts shall find rest. We will be filled with joy, and our mouths shall be full of praise."

In God's will is my peace and joy.

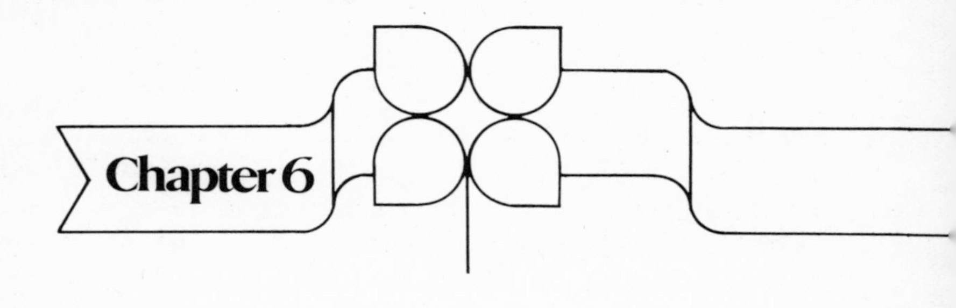

Joy in Blessings

The Lord has done great things for us; we are glad.
Psalm 126:3

Some of the great truths of life may seem commonplace, yet I've learned that there is great strength in these truths. For example, there's the line from an old song, "Count your blessings, name them one by one." Hardly a new idea, yet it becomes new for you if you do it.

I have found that one of the surest ways of releasing God's joy in my life is to stop frequently to give thanks for the blessings of each day, each week, each month, each year. This is for me one of the surest antidotes to depression—concentrating on the blessings I do have rather than worrying about what I don't have. Then I can say with a true heart, "The Lord has done great things for me; I am glad."

It is so easy to forget our blessings and to concentrate on the minor irritations of our lives or on the things we lack. Somehow we have the idea that thinking about the negative aspects of our lives is more "realistic," that concentrating on our blessings seems naive. Yet it is still true that if a glass is

50 percent filled, we can choose to say that the glass is half empty, or we can choose to say that the glass is half full. Both statements are equally realistic, but one perspective will probably depress us, while the other will bring us joy.

Because I am forgetful and easily lose sight of this, I need certain disciplines. One that works for me is to keep a written list of my blessings. This requires me to keep concentrating on them, and it enables me to review when I forget how blessed I am.

When we tally up our blessings, let's not forget the small blessings of each day: a letter or phone call from a friend, a friendly smile from a store clerk, the flowers growing by our doorstep, a hug from a child, a special consideration from a spouse. Dietrich Bonhoeffer wrote, "We pray for big things and forget to give thanks for the ordinary, small (and yet not really small) gifts. How can God entrust great things to one who will not thankfully receive from him the little things?"

But there is no benefit to you just in reading these words. Why not learn the truth of this for yourself? Take a sheet of paper and begin by listing the blessings you enjoy this very day. At the top of your list might be your ability to read and your ability to write such a list. Then think of the blessings of health, of talents, of family, of friends, the blessings of your neighborhood, your house, your state, your country. When so many in the world are faced with war and oppression and terror, think of the protection and peace you enjoy. Then begin to work backwards, remembering the blessings of the past week, the past month, the past year. Then let your mind rove back through your life, thinking of those blessings you especially treasure. It would be surprising if at the end of the list you could not write: "The Lord has done great things for me; I am glad."

To continue to live in this spirit of joyful thanksgiving, re-

12

view this list, and add to it. Maybe you'll want to read it daily or weekly. Review it mentally when you're waiting for a bus, or when you're doing some routine task, or when you're lying in bed awake. God deserves our thanks for all his blessings, and as we give him thanks and concentrate on the gifts he has so richly given us, we will continue to enter into the joy of the Lord.

When we say, "The Lord has done great things for us," we can think not only of the blessings we have received during our lifetime, but we can also remember God's great saving acts in history. We can recall his creation of the universe, his calling of Abraham to be the father of the faithful, his training of the people of Israel to be the bearers of blessing to all nations, his sending his Son to save us from sin and death, and his empowering of the church with the gift of his Holy Spirit. Through the centuries since then he has guided and protected the church, the gathering of believers. He has gifted the church with scholars, poets, musicians, reformers, administrators, preachers, teachers, counselors, and missionaries. As part of the family of God, we share in a "joyful community," one richly blessed by God.

In its fullness, Christian joy goes beyond our blessings to include joy in the midst of trials and persecution and suffering. But we can always return to this simple, obvious, and abiding source of joy—this list of blessings. We can be like Mary, who when she learned that she was to be the mother of the Savior, broke into song and exclaimed, "He who is mighty has done great things for me, and holy is his name." (Luke 1:49).

The Lord has done great things for me; I am glad.

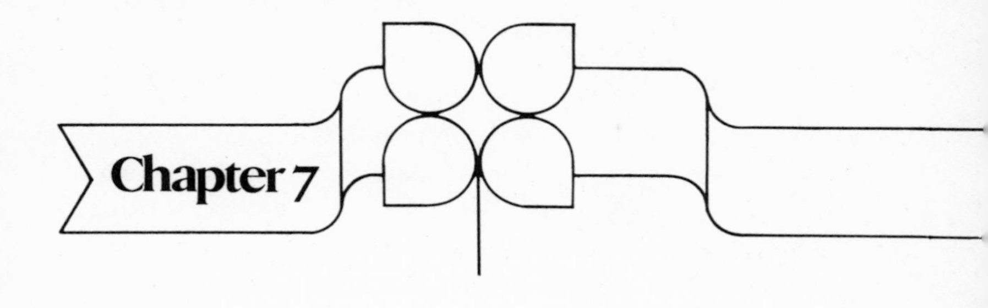

The Greater Joy

Many are asking, "Who can show us any good? Let the light of your face shine upon us, O Lord. You have filled my heart with greater joy than when their grain and new wine abound.
Psalm 4:6-8 NIV

Everyone wants the good life, and there are many forces in our society that try to convince us that the good life means having clothes like the people in the ads or houses like those pictured in the magazines. In the psalmist's day, too, when people looked for the good life, they had in mind grain and wine, wealth and pleasure.

And material blessings are not to be despised. There is no special joy in poverty, especially not the cruel, humiliating poverty which leaves a family without adequate food or shelter or medical care. There is a minimal level of human welfare necessary for normal human happiness, and we have an obligation to see that as many as possible can share in it.

In 1534 Martin Luther wrote to Prince Joachim of Anhalt, who was suffering from depression, advising him to enjoy life and the good things of life: "For honorable and decent joy and good spirits are the best of medicines for a young person, nay, for all people. I, who have spent my former life sorrowing and looking sad, now seek and take joy wherever I can do so. Now we have enough understanding, praise God, to know that we may be happy with a good conscience and may use God's gifts with thanksgiving."

So we do not want to romanticize poverty or despise the good gifts of God given for our joy. But the Bible says that our joy in the Lord is greater than the joy that can come from material things. And sooner or later we find that out. We may begin by seeking joy in things, but when we receive them, we learn that they do not bring the joy we expected.

Why is the joy of material things so limited? For one thing, once we have them, we have to worry about keeping them. Someone buys a house, and then spends his free time maintaining it—or worrying about inflation or property taxes or vandalism. Possessions so quickly become our masters, and we are filled with anxiety lest we lose the things we have. Jesus said it long ago, "Do not lay up for yourselves treasures on earth where moth and rust consume, and where thieves break in and steal. But lay up for yourselves treasures in heaven, where neither moth nor rust consumes and where thieves do not break in and steal. For where your treasure is, there will your heart be also" (Matt. 6:19-21).

We have found some help for our family in the concept of simple living. Simple living means saying no to the forces that encourage us to buy things we don't need to keep up with the Joneses who are buying the same things to keep up with us. But simple living does not mean that we have to live without beauty or graciousness. It does mean learning to live with a *minimum* of things, rather than a maximum. And that minimum is far below what many Americans consider necessary. I say this especially after living in Africa for four years. There we saw people with five percent of the possessions of most Americans, yet they broke into joy and laughter more often than the hard, anxious faces I have seen on the downtown streets of American cities.

Some people have found it helpful, as a step toward simple living, to have a twice-a-year sorting session, going over all possessions—furniture, housewares, clothing, books—and getting rid of whatever is not being used. If you have a "packrat mentality," this may be painful, but when you're finished, you may find joy! Things not being used can be given to people who need them, or they can be sold and the money used for personal or charitable purposes. Many people we know have experienced real joy from this kind of simplifying.

It seems to be a spiritual law that God always gives into our emptiness. As Jesus said, "Blessed are the poor in spirit, for theirs is the kingdom of heaven" (Matt. 5:3). Perhaps one reason why we do not experience the fullness of God's greater joy is that our hearts are already filled—with the desire for things, or with anxiety over preserving the things we have. Even God can't pour more into a full container. A heart empty of the search for material things is empty enough to receive the fullness of God's joy.

That joy will replace the anxiety we may feel about our material needs so that we may experience the truth of Jesus' words: "Therefore do not be anxious, saying, 'What shall we eat?' or 'What shall we drink?' or 'What shall we wear?' For the Gentiles seek all these things; and your heavenly Father knows that you need them all. But seek first his kingdom and his righteousness, and all these things shall be yours as well" (Matt. 6:31-33).

Mine is the greater joy.

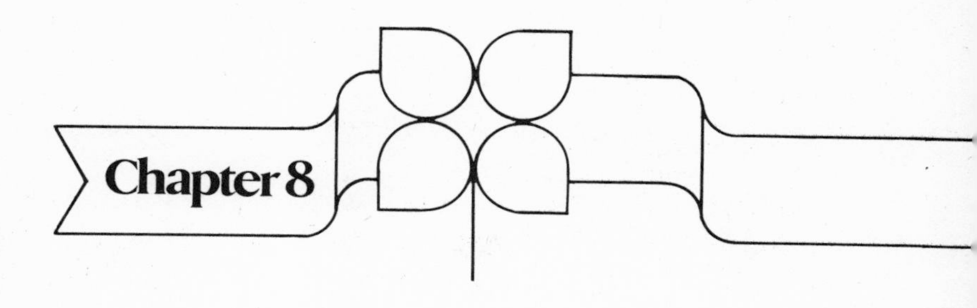

Joy Despite Circumstances

Though the fig tree does not bud,
and there are no grapes on the vines,
though the olive crop fails
and the fields produce no food,
though there are no sheep in the pen,
and no cattle in the stalls,
yet I will rejoice in the Lord,
I will be joyful in God my Savior.

Habakkuk 3:17-18 NIV

Joy is a perfectly natural response when everything is going well, when we are with people we love, when we experience success at our work, when we participate in great moments of beauty in music or art, when our bodies radiate health, when the cupboard of life is full.

But what about the other times, like those painted by Habakkuk? If we could translate his words into the idiom of today, we might say, "Though there is a general recession, and the stock market is down, though prices are up and there's a fuel shortage, and though my weekly check won't reach past

Thursday, "yet I will rejoice in the Lord, I will be joyful in God my Savior."

Habakkuk's joy is not dependent on his outward circumstances but is a joy "in the Lord . . . in God my Savior." The famous missionary to India, E. Stanley Jones, wrote in his autobiography, "I'm a happy man because my happiness is not dependent on happenings, but upon the joy of belonging to him, whatever happens. That is invincible joy." And the British writer William Barclay wrote: "The Christian joy is independent of all things on earth, because the Christian joy has its source in the continual presence of Christ. Two lovers are always happy when they are together, no matter where they are. That is why the Christian can never lose his joy, because he can never lose Jesus Christ."

One reason the Bible is a book people keep coming back to is that it is so realistic. It does not pretend that all is right with the world. It recognizes evil, despair, suffering. It does not pretend they are just illusions. But it does say there is a joy we can experience despite these circumstances.

"Circumstances may at times be anything but conducive to peace or gladness," says Eric Malte. "Yet the believing child of God can always look above and beyond the fitful scenes of earth to the throne where Christ is Ruler of all. His Lord is working in everything for good for those who love Him."

It may not be a major crisis that tempts us to lose our joy. My impression is that people often handle the major crises of life with more strength and poise than one might expect. Perhaps it is just at such times that people stop relying on their own strength and look to God, and he especially bestows his blessing on them because they need it and seek it.

No, it may not be the great tragedy that pulls us down. It may be all the little anxieties, the petty irritations, the trifling worries that rob us of our joy. Therefore it is just in this daily-ness of living that we need to keep God before us. We do that through acts of worship, through daily devotions, through Bible study and prayer, through conversations with family and friends, and through the daily discipline of our thoughts. If we focus on God rather than on circumstances, he will give us his promised joy.

Is this a completely unrealistic, featherheaded approach to life? Stop for a moment and think: Who are the most joyful people you know? (You may find your list is a short one!) Then stop to analyze: Are they the ones who have the most favorable circumstances? If your list is like mine, the answer is no.

I'm thinking of a friend who was drafted into the German army in World War II. Captured by the Russians, he was in a prisoner-of-war camp for several years, so sick and hungry he was reduced to eating the plaster off the walls. Of the people I know, he is one who has suffered more, yet he is one of the most joyful. He is raised above petty irritations and complaints by his gratitude for life and its many little blessings.

People like this—and you can probably think of some—may lack the blessings of a good marriage or a handsome salary or prestige in the world. Yet their joy is not dependent on these circumstances; they have a deep wellspring of joy which grows out of their relationship to God and their commitment to him.

This enables them to say with Habakkuk that big word *yet:* Though the circumstances of life right now are not what I wish, "*yet* I will rejoice in the Lord, I will be joyful in God my Savior."

I will rejoice in the Lord; I will be joyful in God my Savior.

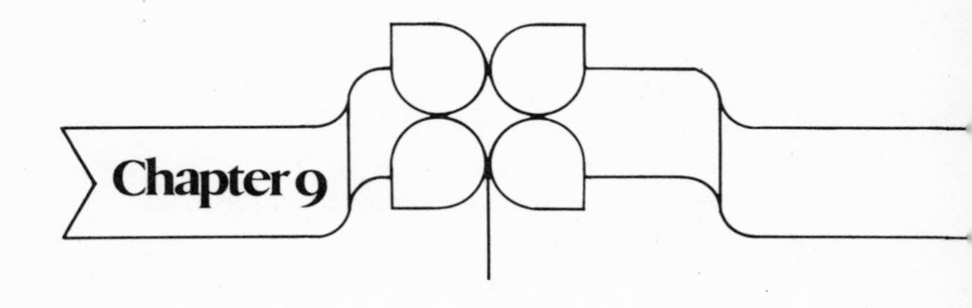

Joy in the Presence of God

You have made known to me the path of life;
you will fill me with joy in your presence,
with eternal pleasures at your right hand.

Psalm 16:11 NIV

My children often ask, "Daddy, where is God?" One of the answers I give is, "God is everywhere." His presence fills the universe, as the psalm writer exclaims, "Where can I go from your Spirit? Where can I flee from your presence? If I go up to the heavens, you are there; if I make my bed in the depths, you are there. If I rise on the wings of the dawn, if I settle on the far side of the sea, even there your hand will guide me, your right hand will hold me fast" (Ps. 139:7-10 NIV).

In one sense we can never escape the presence of God. He will not let us go. Even when we turn from him, his presence follows us. He is the Hound of Heaven who pursues us even when we run from him.

We are always in God's presence, even now. We don't have

to wait for heaven. Jesus said, "Lo, I am with you always, to the close of the age" (Matt. 28:20).

I am sure that every Christian has moments when the presence of God seems real, when it is an experienced reality and not just a promised blessing. Each of us may experience that presence in different ways. Catherine Marshall says, "God deals differently with each of us. He knows no 'typical' case. He seeks us out at a point in our own need and longing and runs down the road to meet us. This individualized treatment should delight rather than confuse us, because it so clearly reveals the highly personal quality of God's love and concern."

For some, the experience of God's presence may come heavily loaded with emotion. For others, it may be a very quiet event, the still, small voice of which Elijah spoke.

Where have you experienced the presence of God? Go to that place regularly. For some it is the quiet, soothing world of nature. For others, God's presence comes most surely when they are studying God's Word. Many feel God most in worship, when the music and setting help to communicate God's presence. For some it will be in quiet moments of solitary prayer. Still others find his presence in deep moments of Christian fellowship, when those gathered get beyond the daily chatter to share from heart to heart and discover God's promise, "Where two or three are gathered in my name, there am I in the midst of them" (Matt. 18:20). If you have experienced the presence of God in a special place, try returning there. It may not work; you may find that "you can't go home again." But it is worth the attempt.

The presence of God as a present reality is always a gift. We cannot force him to provide it at any given moment; there may be reasons why he chooses to withdraw the *experience* of his presence—though not his presence itself. Yet I think he is always more willing to give than we are to receive. While we cannot cause the experience to happen, we can prepare ourselves for it by the ancient and simple discipline of "practicing the presence of God." "Seek the Lord and his strength, seek his presence continually!" says Psalm 105.

A little classic which distills much wisdom about the spiritual life is *Practicing the Presence of God* by Brother Lawrence, a lay brother of the Dominican order who lived in the 16th century. In letters and conversations he tells how he managed, even in his busy practical life in the kitchen or on business trips, to be constantly aware of God's presence. He did this by frequent prayers and thoughts about God, interspersed while he was performing his regular duties.

Brother Lawrence said, "God lays no great burden upon us; a little remembrance of him from time to time, a little adoration, sometimes to pray for his grace, sometimes to offer him your sorrows, and sometimes to return him thanks for the benefits he has given you, and still gives you, in the midst of your troubles. He asks you to console yourself with him the oftenest you can. Lift up your heart to him even at your meals and when you are in company; the least little remembrance will always be acceptable to him. You need not cry very loud; he is nearer to us than we think."

This discipline takes persistent practice as by an act of will we train our minds to think of God often, to turn to him in prayer over all the little things in life. Nothing is too small that it may not become a matter of prayer. As we practice the presence of God, we will learn that he keeps his promise: "Draw near to God and he will draw near to you" (James 4:8).

God is always with us. We know this because he has promised it. This is the bedrock on which our faith rests. Our own experience of his presence, our consciousness of it, may waver. We can, by heartfelt discipline of time and mind, grow in that consciousness. But no matter how disciplined we become, there will probably be moments of darkness when we hang on by faith alone. And when we can no longer hang on, then we can believe that God is hanging on to us. We can even pray like one old saint, "Lord, I shall be very busy today. If I forget thee, do not thou forget me, O Lord."

The joy we feel in God's presence in this life will always be partial, a shadow of things to come, a foretaste of the perfect joy to come. Some day we shall see God face to face, and then we shall rejoice in his presence forevermore.

I rejoice because God is always with me.

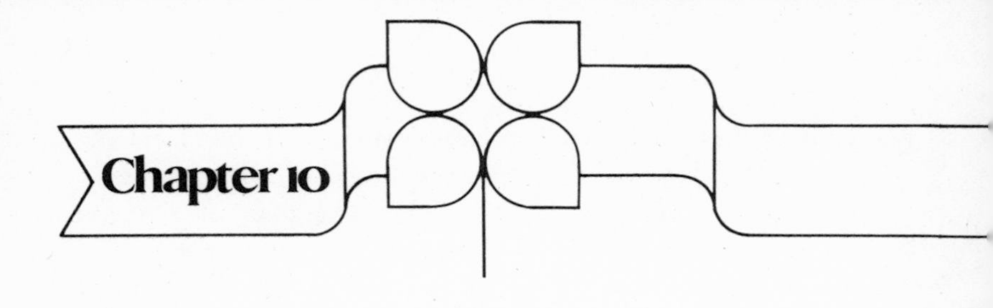

Joy in the Word of God

When your words came, I ate them;
they were my joy and my heart's delight.

Jeremiah 15:16 NIV

As a young teenager I decided it would be good for me to read through the Bible. In a burst of enthusiasm I galloped through Genesis, slogged through Exodus, and became hopelessly bogged down in Leviticus.

There are many people who think the Bible would be good for them. They have been encouraged to read it by pastors and teachers, by family and friends. Yet when they try, they find it confusing rather than helpful, boring rather than exciting. Or the experienced Christian who has read the Bible with profit suddenly may find that the book has seemingly gone stale. There are many who cannot say with the prophet Jeremiah, "When your words came, I ate them; they were my joy and my heart's delight."

Perhaps a few basic principles may help us to *discover* or to *recover* our joy in the Word of God.

1. Read the Bible prayerfully. We are not reading just for information, but for our *formation*. And for that we need the help of the Holy Spirit. Jesus promised us that the Holy Spirit will lead us into all truth (John 16:13); therefore, we should begin our Bible reading by asking the Holy Spirit to be our Teacher. As a thought from the Bible strikes us, we can quickly turn it into a brief prayer. And we can close our reading by asking the Holy Spirit to enable us to put into action the truths we have learned. In this way, our Bible reading will be wrapped in prayer.

2. *Concentrate on those portions of the Bible which offer the greatest spiritual rewards.* "All Scripture is given by inspiration of God and is profitable. . . ." but some parts offer a more immediate blessing than others. We will probably want to major in the New Testament, concentrating on the life of Jesus in Matthew, Mark, Luke, and John, then going on to the letters of Paul and the other apostles. In the Old Testament you will probably find that the Psalms and the Prophets will speak most directly to your life.

3. *Don't just read; expect to study.* In the interest of encouraging Bible reading, some people have made the Bible sound easy. Parts of it are. Martin Luther compared the Bible to a river. Near the banks a little baby can sit and splash. But in the middle an elephant can drown. Especially for beginners, the Bible may seem like an alien book, an odd collection of ancient history, poetry, sermons, letters, songs, wise sayings, dreams, and visions. The Bible requires more than casual reading. It may take real study—alone or in a group—for you to experience the joy that is to be found in this Book.

4. *Try a variety of translations.* After nearly 300 years during which the King James Version of the Bible held sway over the English-speaking Protestant world, we are now blessed with an abundance of 20th-century translations. If you've been accustomed to reading the King James or Revised

Standard versions, you may find that the Bible takes on new freshness if you switch to the Good News Bible, or the New International Version, or one of the free paraphrases like Phillips.

5. *Follow the ancient precept and "Read, mark, learn, and inwardly digest" the words of the Bible.* As we read our way through a book of the Bible, we can mark those verses which especially speak to our condition. Many have discovered the blessing that comes from learning these verses by memory. If we have committed a verse to memory, we can reflect on it throughout the day. Dietrich Bonhoeffer, the Lutheran pastor martyred by the Nazis in World War II, wrote, "The Word of Scripture should never stop sounding in your ears and working in you all day long, just like the words of someone you love. And just as you do not analyze the words of someone you love, but accept them as they are said to you, accept the Word of Scripture and ponder it in your heart as Mary did."

As we ponder the Word of Scripture, we try to see especially how it applies to our life. It's no good reading the Bible just for information, or for proof texts to use against those who disagree with us. It is only when the Word is internalized as the Word of God to me that it will bear fruit in my life. As I read and ponder, I need to ask, "What is the Holy Spirit saying to me today?" It is this process of internalizing that Jeremiah had in mind when he said, "When your words came, I ate them; they were my joy and my heart's delight."

6. *Do not read the Bible expecting emotional thrills.* I believe that the fruit of Bible study is joy, but it is more likely to appear when we are not striving after it. And even the greatest Christians testify to periods of dryness. It is important that we stick to our reading and study, even when we don't feel like it or when the emotional reward seems to be

missing. Elizabeth O'Connor, in *A Search for Silence,* stresses this need for persistence in our use of God's Word: "To take a book of the Bible, to immerse one's self in it and be grasped by it, is to have one's life literally revolutionized. This requires study and the training of our attention. The student stays with it through barren day after barren day, until at last the meaning is clear, and transformation happens."

When it happens, you will be able to say with the psalmist, "Your statutes are my heritage forever; they are the joy of my heart" (Ps. 119:111 NIV).

God's Word is my joy and my heart's delight.

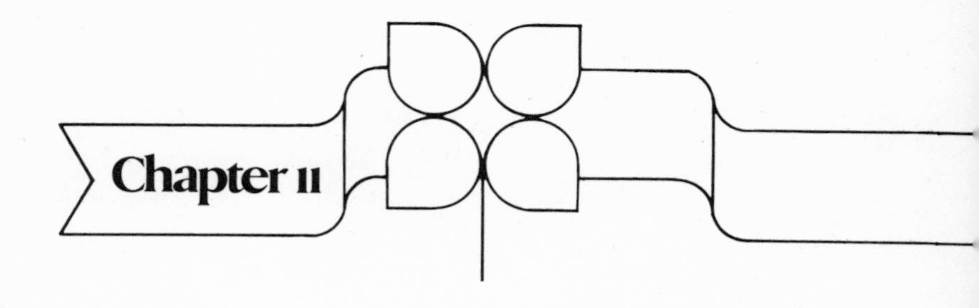

Joy in Meditation

My soul is feasted as with marrow and fat,
and my mouth praises thee with joyful lips,
when I think of thee upon my bed,
and meditate on thee in the watches of the night;
for thou hast been my help,
and in the shadow of thy wings I sing for joy.

Psalm 63:5-7

I used to be into meditation," a long-haired young man said to me. "But then I found Jesus." His implication was plain: meditation was something one did before becoming a Christian; it was not something Christians did. For many, the word *meditation* conjures up a picture of an Indian guru, sitting cross-legged, hands folded in lap, eyes closed in dreamy reverie.

But meditation is for Christians. Meditation is a good biblical word, and the Bible presents meditation as one of our sources of joy. God told Joshua, "This book of the law shall not depart out of your mouth, but you shall *meditate* on it day and night, that you may be careful to do according to all that is written in it; for then you shall make your way prosperous, and then you shall have good success" (Josh. 1:8). The psalm writers said, "I will *meditate* on all your works and consider all your mighty deeds" (Ps. 77:12 NIV), and "I meditate on your precepts and consider your ways. I delight in your decrees; I will not neglect your word" (Ps. 119:15-16 NIV).

What is meditation? J. I. Packer, in his book *Knowing God,* defines it this way: "Meditation is the activity of calling to mind, and thinking over, and dwelling on and applying to oneself, the various things that one knows about the works and ways and purposes and promises of God. . . . It is a matter of talking to oneself about God and oneself; it is, indeed, often a matter of arguing with oneself, reasoning oneself out of moods of doubt and unbelief into a clear apprehension of God's power and grace."

In the heat of summer, a sudden, drenching thunderstorm does a garden little good. The water runs off the hard ground without soaking in. A long, slow drizzle, what my father calls "a good rain," is what the garden needs. We sometimes need "a good rain" in a spiritual sense. In meditation we take enough time to let the Word of God soak into our minds and be absorbed into our lives.

We can meditate at any quiet time—lying in bed, riding on the bus, walking to a store, doing routine household tasks. But two times of day are especially important for meditation. Leslie Weatherhead wrote, "It is almost impossible to exaggerate the importance of the last thoughts at night and the first thoughts in the morning. Our fathers and mothers, who taught us to say our prayers night and morning, were wiser psychologists than they knew. The ideas that are dominant in the mind when the mind is quiescent are the most determinative ideas of the personality."

The tradition of a "morning watch" is a revered one. The writer of Psalm 119 said, "I rise before dawn and cry for help; I have put my hope in your word. My eyes stay open through the watches of the night, that I may meditate on your promises" (vv. 147-48 NIV). In our morning devotions we may read a chapter of the Bible, stopping to reflect on a verse that especially speaks to us. We need not strain our thinking; we can relax and let our minds dwell on a thought as if handling a fine piece of china, turning it over carefully, looking at it from one angle and then another. We can try to apply the verse to our own life and then just let it soak into our consciousness to become a part of us. It may be helpful to memorize a verse that has special meaning so we can meditate on it throughout the day.

Have you ever spent a restless night, with anxious, unbidden thoughts robbing you of sleep's release? You send the anxious thoughts away, but before you know it, they're back. All you can think about is how tired you will be the next day. Compare this with the joyful experience of the psalmist: "I think of thee upon my bed, and meditate on thee in the watches of the night."

At one time I found myself wishing for more quiet time in the day, time free from the demands of job and family, time I could use for prayer and meditation. At the same time I was troubled with insomnia. Then I realized God was giving me the quiet time I needed—in the middle of the night when the house was still. So I began to use the time for meditation. The only problem was that soon my insomnia evaporated!

Whether in the morning or the night or the time between, we can try to practice what Paul suggested to the Christians at Philippi: "Finally, brethren, whatever is true, whatever is honorable, whatever is just, whatever is pure, whatever is lovely, whatever is gracious, if there is any excellence, if there is anything worthy of praise, think about these things" (Phil. 4:8).

The psalmist promises the benefits of such meditation. First, "My soul is feasted as with marrow and fat." Now to us who are calorie-conscious, the picture of fat and marrow may not have immediate appeal, but it was a good Old Testament way of talking about being well-fed. We give much thought to seeing that our families are well-nourished in body, because we know that a diet of junk food can weaken a body and make it susceptible to disease. There is junk food of the mind too—trivial, fretful, anxious, polluted thoughts which crowd out the thoughts of God and weaken our souls. Instead of mental junk food, we can let our minds feast on the things of God.

The psalmist also says, "My mouth praises thee with joyful lips." A heart filled with the thoughts of God spills over into songs of joy.

I meditate on the things of God, and I am filled with joy.

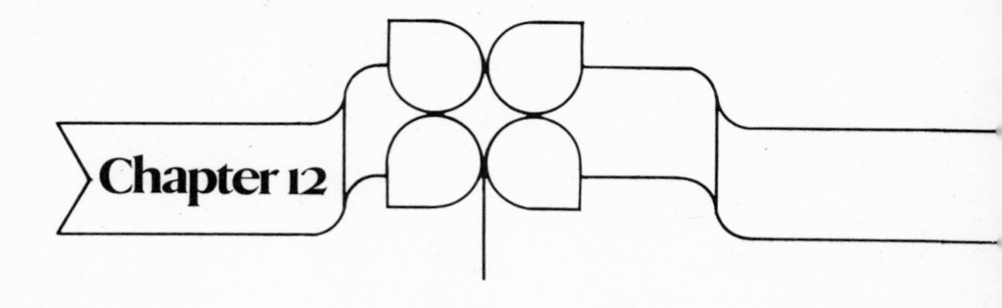

Fresh Joy for the Meek

The meek shall obtain fresh joy in the Lord.

Isaiah 29:19

From the richness of Egypt, Moses led the children of Israel out of slavery, through the Sinai peninsula, a barren desert. Here God provided food for them by a daily miracle. They went out in the morning and found the ground covered with small round wafers that tasted like honey. It was manna. And every morning, except the sabbath day of rest, they could go out and gather a fresh supply of this heavenly bread. But if they attempted to keep any overnight—perhaps because they were not confident of a fresh supply—it turned rotten and decayed. They needed a fresh supply of manna every morning. God promised it, and he provided it.

He promises us fresh joy. And we need fresh joy, because no emotion lasts. It is normal in life that we have some mountaintop experiences, times when God feels especially near, or when we experience the power of the Holy Spirit, or when we are lost in adoration. But it is also normal for those emotions to fade, and any attempt to sustain them is sure to lead to frustration.

C. S. Lewis says, "It is simply no good trying to keep any thrill; that is the very worst thing you can do. Let the thrill go—let it die away—go on through that period of death into the quieter interest and happiness that follow. And you will find that you are living in a world of new thrills all the time." That is "fresh joy in the Lord."

This fresh joy is promised to the *meek*. What picture does that word conjure up for you? Is it the henpecked husband, capable only of heroic dreams, like Walter Mitty? Is it the sniveling Uriah Heep, groveling and scraping before his superiors? Is it the shy wallflower or the patient doormat? With that understanding, it's hard to imagine how Jesus' words could come true: "Blessed are the meek, for they shall inherit the earth" (Matt. 5:5).

We would come closer to the biblical meaning of *meek* if we translated it as "the teachable" or "the disciplined." "The *teachable* shall obtain fresh joy in the Lord." "Blessed are the *disciplined,* for they shall inherit the earth."

The meek, then, are not those who think they know it all, but those who are continually searching, not those who have all the answers, but those who are always learning. These shall obtain fresh joy in the Lord.

The word *discipline* is related to the word *disciple,* meaning learner. So if we are really to be disciples of Jesus, we must be continually learning, not just religious information, but ways of living.

How are we to be disciplined learners before God? Let's admit that it's not easy. The conflicting demands of family, friends, church, and society can fragment our lives, making us feel that we are being pulled in all directions at the same time. Television commercials may encourage us to expect instant solutions to all our problems. Magazine articles may direct us to "do your own thing," which may mean choosing the self-indulgent option or the one that requires the least effort on our part.

Confronted by these pressures, needs, and options, we need discipline in our lives if we are to achieve the potential to which God calls us. Let's think briefly of discipline in three areas of our lives.

1. Discipline of the body. From the studies of psychosomatic medicine we have learned much about the interrelatedness of body and spirit. To reach our potential of joy we must discipline our bodies. We need to eat the right kinds of food and not abuse our bodies with junk foods or alcohol or unnecessary drugs. And our joy in life can be increased by the right amounts of physical exercise and sleep.

2. Discipline of the mind. We are commanded to love the Lord with all our minds, and we are instructed to bring every thought captive in obedience to Christ (2 Cor. 10:5). This calls for a constant watch, refusing to dwell on those thoughts which kill our joy, but concentrating on positive thoughts which nurture our joy. Ralph Waldo Emerson said, "A man is what he thinks about all day long." And William Lyon Phelps wrote, "The happiest person is the person who thinks the most interesting thoughts."

3. Discipline of the spirit. Here we think of the devotional life—regular reading of the Bible, memorization of Scripture, meditation on the Word of God, continuing faithfulness in prayer. Without this, it simply is not possible to receive or to maintain the joy of the Lord.

Our attempts at discipline may falter—mine often do. But we can keep coming back, knowing we are forgiven and restored. His mercies are new every morning. Strengthened by his forgiveness, we can each day pursue our disciplined way and discover for ourselves how the meek obtain fresh joy in the Lord.

I obtain fresh joy in the Lord.

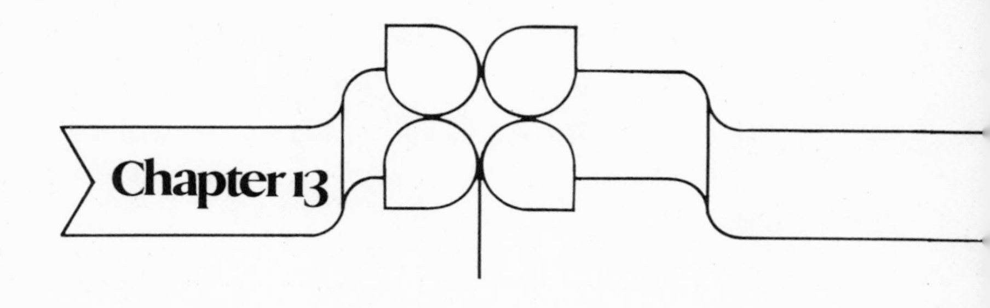

Joy at the Altar

Send forth your light and your truth, let them guide me;
let them bring me to your holy mountain,
to the place where you dwell.
Then will I go to the altar of God,
to God, my joy and my delight.
I will praise you with the harp,
O God, my God.

Psalm 43:3-4 NIV

Bible scholars tell us that Psalms 42 and 43 were originally one psalm; we can see this in the repeated refrain: "Why are you downcast, O my soul? Why so disturbed within me? Put your hope in God; for I will yet praise him, my savior and my God."

The opening words of Psalm 42 picture a person who is feeling anything but joy: "As the deer pants for streams of water, so my soul pants for you, O God. My soul thirsts for God, for the living God. When can I go and meet with God? My tears have been my food day and night, while men say to me all day long, 'Where is your God?'" Here is someone who longs to feel the presence of God but is surrounded by scoffers who mock the faith. In the midst of this joylessness, the psalm writer remembers a time of great joy: a trip to Jerusalem for one of the great religious festivals. It was a joyful experience, going "with the multitude, leading the procession to the house of God, with shouts of joy and thanksgiving among the festive throng." Psalm 43 is a prayer asking God to once again grant the experience of the joy of worship with fellow believers: "Send forth your light and your truth, let them guide me; let them bring me to your holy mountain, to the place where you dwell. Then will I go to the altar of God, to God, my joy and delight."

This psalm points us to one of the sources of our joy in the Lord, the joy of joining in worship with other believers before the altar of God.

Like the psalm writer, each of us can probably remember some high points in our life of worship. For some it may be the memory of Christmas Eve services as a child. It may be the memory of worshiping in the splendor of a great cathedral with a majestic choir and organ. It may have been a quiet moment of sharing around a campfire at Bible camp, or a simple service in a white-frame country church.

These moments are precious gifts from God, and it is good for us to treasure them, to remember them, to relive them in our imaginations, as did the psalmist. Psychologists refer to these as peak experiences, those special moments when we feel truly alive and harmonious and filled with meaning.

Our worship life, however, is not normally a continual series of mountain peaks. There are probably valleys—or even pits. There may be moments when we feel as Robert Louis Stevenson did when he wrote in his journal: "Went to church today; was not too depressed." If you have found a church where joy is present and expressed in worship, thank

God and rejoice in it. If you have not, you may be able to help provide it, at least by your own example.

It does seem to me that in the last few years many churches are learning that worship can be solemn and reverent and at the same time have a dominant note of joy. I remember when that was not the case. As a child I was impressed by the solemnity of worship, especially the communion service. As the people walked up to the altar, the organist would play mournful music, and people who were normally happy would put on very sad faces. Returning from the altar, they would be careful to look at the floor and to avoid smiling. Now we can see that communion at God's table can also be thought of as a time of joy, when we come to meet God and to celebrate our fellowship with him and with one another.

Not so very long ago, when guitars and folk hymns were still new to many churches, I had played guitar and taught some lively folk hymns to the young people of my congregation. When I asked the pastor whether the young people might sing them in church, he was hesitant. He wasn't at all sure about those songs, especially accompanied by guitar. He finally agreed—on one condition: if we were sure that not one of the young people would *smile* during the songs!

Mother Basilea Schlink has said, "No wonder the masses of men, God's creatures, prefer to go to the woods and parks on Sunday. There in the midst of the creation of God, they experience something of the joy and beauty which nature reflects. This gives them a bit of joy that every human heart longs for. When they go to church, they often do not sense any joy, they do not see it on the faces, they do not find the radiance of God in the churches as they do out in nature. Where do they hear joyful singing in the churches? Where do they sense that the hearts are really singing along, so that their hearts will also be swept along to joy in their Lord Jesus Christ?"

At the same time that we point out the need for joy in our worship, we should recognize a danger. There is a kind of spiritual hypochondria that keeps taking its own spiritual temperature. If we keep looking at ourselves to ask, "Am I being joyful now?" our attention is focused on ourselves, on our joy, rather than on God who is the source of our joy. We come to worship, not to seek joy, but to seek God. Joy, when it comes, comes as a by-product, not as something sought. The more we lose ourselves in God, the more likely we are to find the joy of worship.

I will go to the altar of God, to God, my joy and my delight.

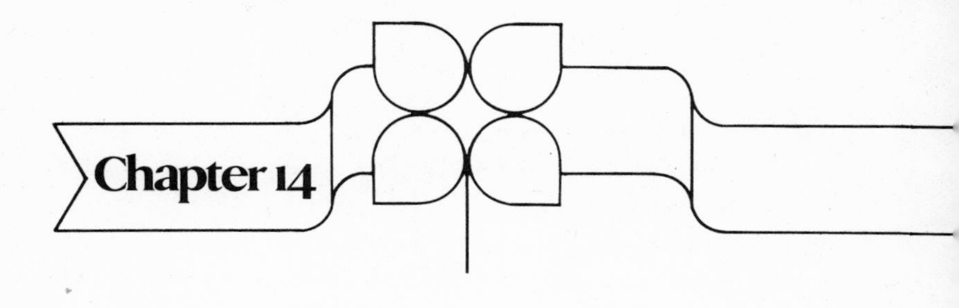

The Joy of Christmas

And the angel said to them, "Be not afraid; for behold, I bring you good news of a great joy which will come to all the people; for to you is born this day in the city of David a Savior, who is Christ the Lord."

Luke 2:10-11

It was a sweltering Sunday morning in July when our pastor announced that the opening hymn would be "Joy to the World." I found it hard to muster as much enthusiasm as he wished, yet I knew he was right: The joy of Christmas is not meant to be limited to one day or a few weeks in the year. It is for all of life.

The first Christmas 2000 years ago was circled with joy. The joy of Mary and Joseph at the birth of their first baby. The joy of the shepherds as they heard the angel announce "good news of a great joy which will come to all the people." The joy of the Wise Men when the star led them to the infant King. It was a joyous moment in time, the fulfillment of the expectations and hopes of Israel, as God's Son entered our world to redeem all people.

If we think of any season of the year as joyful, it is Christmas. " 'Tis the season to be jolly" blares out in every department store and supermarket. Yet our "falalalala" may ring hollow. Psychologists report that Christmas is one of the worst seasons for depression. They say that we try too hard to be joyful. We ask too much of this one season, expecting it to provide enough joy to make up for the rest of the year. Some people exhaust themselves at partying, trying too desperately to be happy, and the hangover from too much food and too much drink leaves no space for joy. Still others are saddened at Christmas by the memories of happier circumstances in the past.

The first Christmas was not perfect either. There was much that was not outwardly joyous. Palestine lay under the harsh domination of conquering Rome, the people groaning under the oppression and longing for national freedom. The baby was not born in the comfort of a palace—or even an inn—but in the cold and dirt of a barn. As far as we know, Mary, probably a very young girl, gave birth to her first baby without benefit of a midwife and with only her frightened husband to assist. And within days they had to flee the slaughtering hand of Herod.

So the joy which the angels sang about was not "God's in his heaven; all's right with the world." Everything was not all right then—and it's not all right now. Nevertheless, we can still know the joy of Christmas.

One year when we were teaching at a school for missionary children in Madagascar, some of our students were not able to go home for Christmas because their travel visas had not arrived. The students were crushed at the thought of being separated from their families at Christmas, and we all shared in their disappointment. As we planned a Christmas service, we said, "It's not going to be easy for us to sing 'Joy to the

World' this Christmas." Then someone said, "Well, we can't sing, 'Joy to the world, the *visas* have come,' but we still can sing, 'Joy to the world, the *Lord* is come.' That hasn't changed, and that is our cause for rejoicing."

In order to appreciate the joy of Christmas we must look for joy in the right place. We cannot look for it in "a white Christmas, just like the ones we used to know" because it may not snow. We cannot look for it in gifts and overindulgent meals because these bring no lasting happiness. We cannot even look for it in the warmth of friends or family, because these are not always with us. We look for the joy of Christmas in the baby in the manger; if we do not find it there, we never will find it.

The meaning of that joy is wrapped up in one of the baby's names. He is called Immanuel, which means "God with us." For the joy of Christmas lies in the fact that God has come into our history to be with us, to show us what love is, to demonstrate what it means to be fully human. The poet Christina Rossetti wrote, "Love came down at Christmas."

But the message of Christmas is in the present tense: not God *was* with us, but God *is* with us. He is not with us in the same way as he was in the baby of Bethlehem, but he is with us as he pours love and strength and comfort into our hearts. Not everyone knows this experience, this presence of Jesus, for God does not force himself into our hearts. At that first Christmas God did not force the innkeeper to receive his Son. So we too may shut the doors of our heart and say, "No room." Or we can pray in the words of Martin Luther:

> Ah dearest Jesus, holy child,
> Make thee a bed, soft undefiled,
> Within my heart that it may be
> A quiet chamber kept for thee.

And we can do this at any time of year. We can do it right now. No matter what the season, we can know the great joy which is for all people.

I rejoice because God is with us.

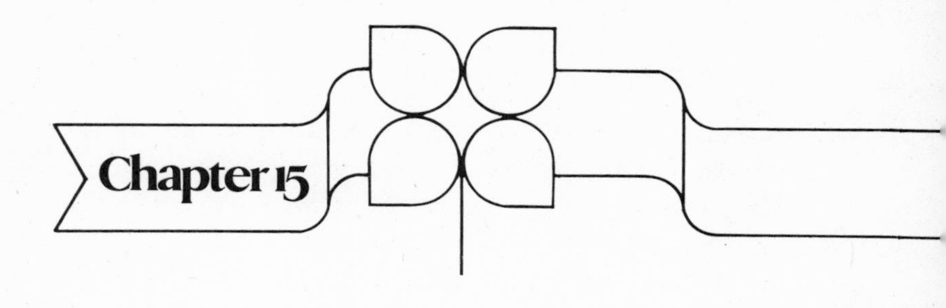

The Joy of Easter

So they departed quickly from the tomb with fear and great joy, and ran to tell his disciples.

Matthew 28:8

Perhaps some of the most joyless hearts the world has ever known were those of the sorrowing women who trudged their tedious way to the tomb of their crucified Lord, all their hopes drowned in their own tears. They came for the sad task of embalming the body of the one they had loved and in whom they had placed all their hopes. He had been the center of their lives and their loves and their dreams. Now he lay dead, and their hopes were dead with him.

But the God of surprises had a great surprise in store for them. At the tomb an angelic messenger stunned them with the announcement, "He is not here; for he has risen, as he said. Come, see the place where he lay. Then go quickly and tell his disciples that he has risen from the dead, and behold, he is going before you to Galilee; there you will see him (Matt. 28:6-7). With that announcement, the women's sorrow was transformed into joy. "They departed quickly from the tomb with fear and great joy."

Jesus then appeared to the women, to his 11 remaining disciples, and to a group of 500 believers who were alive at the time of Paul and could testify that they had seen Jesus. The early Christians were convinced of one thing: Jesus did not remain in the grave; he was alive again to live forever. This was the message they carried as they went out into the pagan world: Christ is risen!

For nearly 2000 years believers have come to the same conclusion: that Jesus is still a living Savior. William Barclay summarizes the joyful benefits of Christ's resurrection: "In every problem the risen Christ is there to consult, in every effort he is there to help. In every sorrow he is there to comfort. On every dark road he is there to banish fear, and in the sunshine he is there to make joy doubly dear."

Easter means that we have a living Savior who has promised, "Lo, I am with you always, to the close of the age" (Matt. 28:20). Easter means that death is not our greatest enemy, the end of all our hopes and relationships. For death has been conquered. In the continuing life of Jesus we can see that God is stronger than death.

In our lives we may experience death in many ways—not just the death of our bodies, but the death of relationships, projects, plans, organizations, programs, cherished dreams. Yet God can always bring life out of death. If we do not hang on to the thing that has died, if we release it and go on in life, God can move us on to new life, new relationships, new work, new dreams, new hopes. Paul speaks of this life-giving power of God in our lives when he says, "I ask that your minds may be opened to see his light, so that you will know what is the hope to which he has called you, how rich are the wonderful blessings he promises his people, and how very great is his

power at work in us who believe. This power working in us is the same as the mighty strength which he used when he raised Christ from death" (Eph. 1:18-20 TEV).

One way that the Bible describes the benefits of Easter for us is to say that Easter gives us eternal life. When I was younger, I thought this meant only that when I die, God will raise me to live with him forever. It does mean that. But eternal life is not a *quantity* of life, but a *quality* of life. It is God's life lived in us and through us, something that is already happening to us now. Phillips Brooks wrote: "The great Easter truth is not that we are to live newly after death—that is not the great thing—but that we are to be new here and now by the power of the resurrection, not so much that we are to live forever as that we are to, and may, live nobly now because we are to live forever."

One of the most moving stories I have read about the power of God to bring life out of death is Ernest Gordon's *Through the Valley of the Kwai.* In it he tells of the incredible suffering that British prisoners of war endured as they labored to build the bridge over the River Kwai for the Japanese. Their lives were encompassed by starvation, disease, torture, and the dangers of the jungle. Yet at a time when they were reduced nearly to the level of animals, a few Christians began practicing the love of God, caring for one another, sharing the Bible, praying together. The life of the prison camps was transformed. Gordon describes an early morning Easter celebration shortly before the end of the war: "At dawn on Easter some of us slipped out of our huts to make our communion in the open at the edge of the camp. There we received the elements in token of our Lord's sacrifice, that we might be strengthened to follow 'the Comrade-God who on the cross was slain, to rise again.' When we finished, the sun was up. The darkness was still here, but it was being overcome by light. Death was here, but it was being redeemed by life, God's life."

Like the joy of Christmas, the joy of Easter is not limited to one season of the year. We can celebrate Easter daily as we die to sin and rise to new life, for it is the risen Christ who lives in us and through us, as Paul wrote: "It is no longer I who live, but Christ who lives in me" (Gal. 2:20). This new life was guaranteed for us when God raised Jesus from the dead, demonstrating for all time that Jesus paid the sacrifice for our sin, that the power of death over us is broken, that God's love is always stronger than death.

Peter sums up our Easter hope: "Let us give thanks to the God and Father of our Lord Jesus Christ! Because of his great mercy he gave us new life by raising Jesus Christ from death. This fills us with a living hope, and so we look forward to possessing the rich blessings that God keeps for his people" (1 Peter 1:3-4 TEV).

I rejoice in new life.

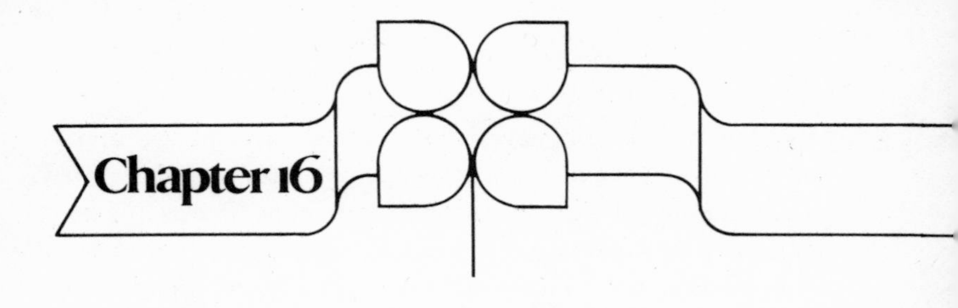

The Joy of Believing

May the God of hope fill you with all joy and peace in believing, so that by the power of the Holy Spirit you may abound in hope.

Romans 15:13

Martin Luther made a close connection between our faith and our joy when he said, "We can mark our lack of faith by our joy; for our joy must necessarily be as great as our faith." Luther is saying: great faith, great joy; little faith, little joy. Paul also made the connection between faith and joy: "May the God of hope fill you with all joy and peace in believing." So if we are not experiencing the fullness of joy, we can look to our faith.

What is faith? No better definition exists than that in the book of Hebrews: "Now faith is the assurance of things hoped for, the conviction of things not seen" (11:1). Farther on in Hebrews 11 we read, "Without faith it is impossible to please him. For whoever would draw near to God must believe that he exists and that he rewards those who seek him" (v. 6). From our side, faith means being open to the idea that God exists, acting as if he exists, and then awaiting his response.

This means there is always an element of risk in believing, always a sense in which we are betting our lives that there is a God. When we float in water, we have to take our feet off the bottom and entrust ourselves to the lifting power of the waves. In the same way, we have to let go of our doubts and anxieties and trust God. When that happens, we know the joy and peace of believing.

Faith is the opposite of sight, of absolute evidence. When Jesus appeared to his disciples behind locked doors on the first Easter evening, Thomas was absent. When the other disciples gave him the exciting news that Jesus was alive again, Thomas responded, "Unless I see in his hands the print of the nails, and place my finger in the mark of the nails, and place my hand in his side, I will not believe" (John 20:25). A week later, Jesus appeared to his disciples again, this time with Thomas present. Thomas did touch the wounds of Jesus and was convinced. But Jesus said to him, "Blessed are those who have not seen and yet believe" (20:29). Peter wrote about Jesus, "Without having seen him you love him; though you do not now see him you believe in him and rejoice with unutterable and exalted joy" (1 Peter 1:8).

How do we get faith if we don't have it? I will suggest four steps:

1. Ask for it. Faith is a gift of God, not something we achieve. A man once came to Jesus seeking healing for his son. Jesus said to him, "All things are possible to him who believes" (Mark 9:23). The man responded, "I believe; help my unbelief." Or another translation reads, "I do have faith, but not enough. Help me have more!" This points to the double action we can take: we can live by the faith we have, and we can ask God to increase our faith.

2. *Associate with people who have faith.* Faith is *caught* rather than taught. I once heard a speaker addressing a group of university students about the Christian faith. A student in the audience asked, "If I don't have faith, how can I get it?" The speaker answered, "Find some people who have it, and be with them."

I suppose that faith has never been easy, but it seems particularly hard in our day when so many values are being questioned, when so many are unsure about what to believe, when so many traditional teachings and practices are being challenged and changed. It is no wonder people are left with the question, "What can I believe?" We need people with whom we can share our doubts, air our questions, and with whom we can seek truth and faith.

3. *Immerse yourself in the teachings of the Bible.* Paul said, "Faith comes from what is heard, and what is heard comes by the preaching of Christ" (Rom. 10:17). Down through history faithful Christians have testified that the source of their faith was the Bible. Through the Scriptures the Holy Spirit works faith in our hearts. As we read about what God has done for others, when we study the lives of people of faith, we are encouraged to venture forward in faith.

4. *Live by the faith you have.* Every day gives us opportunities to trust God where we can and to obey him as we see our duty. George Macdonald wrote, "Instead of asking yourself whether you believe or not, ask yourself whether you have this day done one thing because He said, *Do it,* or once abstained because He said, *Do not do it.* It is simply absurd to say you believe in Him, if you do not do anything He tells you." As we live in obedience to God, and as we exercise the faith we have, our faith will grow.

We can take these four steps then—and take them over and over. We can pray, "Lord, increase my faith." We can seek out the fellowship of those who have faith, and we can learn with them and from them. We can immerse ourselves in the Bible, through which the Holy Spirit works faith. And we can live in obedience to the faith we have. As we do these things, the God of hope will fill us with all joy and peace in believing.

I believe, and I am filled with joy and peace.

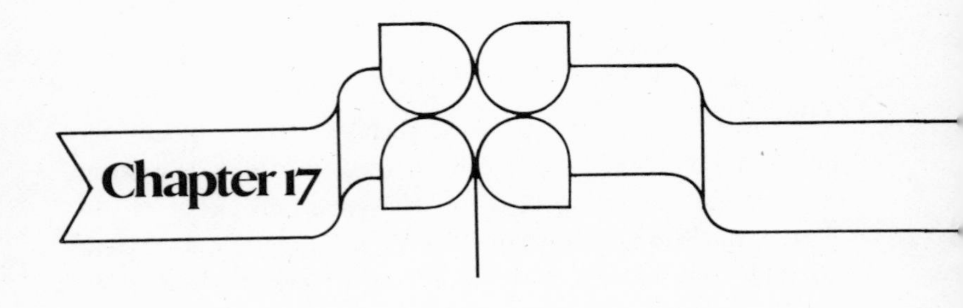

Joy Always

Rejoice always, pray constantly, give thanks in all circumstances; for this is the will of God in Christ Jesus for you.

1 Thessalonians 5:16-18

"Rejoice always." For a long time I have stumbled over that verse. Is it really possible? Can one be joyful all the time? How can that be in the face of personal problems, and national problems, and world problems? Rejoice always? Isn't that unrealistic?

Who is it that said, "Rejoice always"? It must have been some Pollyanna, someone who lived a sheltered life, free from the evils and anxieties that press in on us from all sides.

No, these are not the words of Pollyanna, but the words of Paul. Did he live a sheltered life, free from problems and dangers? Listen to his summary: "Five times I was given the thirty-nine lashes by the Jews; three times I was whipped by the Romans; and once I was stoned. I have been in three shipwrecks, and once spent twenty-four hours in the water. In my many travels I have been in danger from floods and from robbers, in danger from fellow Jews and from Gentiles; there have been dangers in the cities, dangers in the wilds, dangers on the high seas, and dangers from false friends. There has been work and toil; often I have gone without sleep; I have been hungry and thirsty; I have often been without enough food, shelter, or clothing. And not to mention other things, every day I am under the pressure of my concern for all the churches. When someone is weak, then I feel weak too; when someone is led into sin, I am filled with distress" (2 Cor. 11:24-29 TEV).

That is the life history of a believer who said, "Rejoice always." We recognize that Paul is far ahead of us on the road of faith, yet if God can make Paul rejoice always, then he can also give us the gift of joy. For with God, nothing is impossible.

Is there any secret as to how we can rejoice always? Maybe there is a clue in the words following Paul's encouragement; he goes on to say, "Pray constantly" and "Give thanks in all circumstances."

When we speak of giving thanks in all circumstances, we must speak with great care, especially when giving advice to one who is suffering. What comes to us happens with God's permission, but we should not speak in a way that makes God the cause of evil.

I have heard a man say that when he was hit by a truck, as he was flying through the air, he exclaimed, "Thank you, God, for sending that truck to hit me." I have heard of others who have said, "Thank you, Lord, for this cancer." I think that these words must never be spoken lightly, and, in particular, we should never glibly urge them on others. Isaiah says, "Woe to those who call evil good and good evil" (5:20). Baron von Hügel said, "Evil is a mystery, and you can't do away with it by calling it good."

Yet we can always say this: "We know that in everything God works for good with those who love him" (Rom. 8:28). Even when evil happens to us, we can rejoice and thank God that he is at work in the situation to bring about our good.

I do not believe that God wishes evil on us, not ever. I am a father, and I can't imagine a father who wants his children to have cancer or to be injured in a traffic accident or to starve to death. But I can identify with a father who in the midst of a tragedy is there, offering his strength and comfort.

In *The Hiding Place* Corrie ten Boom tells how she and her sister Betsie were captured for helping Jews escape the Nazis. Corrie and Betsie were then sent to the dread German concentration camp Ravensbruck. As they were led into the huge barracks filled with large platforms holding hundreds of prisoners, they were horrified at the filth, the fetid air, the wretched quarters. They flopped down on some reeking straw mattresses, overcome with nausea, only to find the mats swarming with fleas. Corrie cried out, "Betsie, how can we live in such a place?"

Betsie answered with Paul's words, "Give thanks in all circumstances."

So they begin to give thanks for the fact that they were together, for their Bible, for the many people who could hear their gospel message. But when Betsie went on to give thanks for the fleas, Corrie thought, "This is too much. There is no way even God can make me grateful for fleas."

"Give thanks in *all* circumstances," Betsie repeated. "It doesn't say 'in pleasant circumstances.' Fleas are part of this place where God has put us."

"And so we stood between piers of bunks," Corrie recounts, "and gave thanks for fleas. But this time I was sure Betsie was wrong."

It was later that the sisters learned why they were never

disturbed by the guards as they taught the Bible and counseled and prayed with the other prisoners. The guards had been afraid to enter the barracks—because of the fleas!

A God who can cause a Paul or a Corrie ten Boom to rejoice and give thanks in all circumstances can also make it possible for us. We can begin by giving thanks for all the good things in our lives and trusting him to bring good even out of the hardships we are experiencing. We can live out the words of Paul in Philippians 4:4: "Rejoice in the Lord always; again I will say, Rejoice. . . . Have no anxiety about anything, but in everything by prayer and supplication with thanksgiving let your requests be made known to God."

I rejoice in the Lord always.

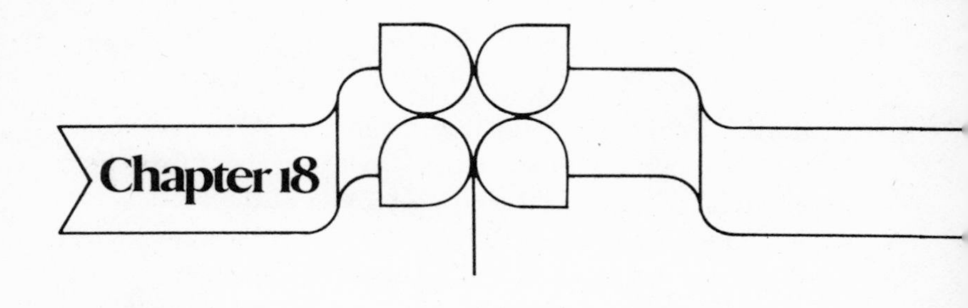

The Joy of Prayer

Ask, and you will receive, that your joy may be full.

John 16:24

For me one of the saddest phrases in the Bible is, "You do not have because you do not ask" (James 4:2). One of the reasons we do not experience the fullness of God's joy is that we do not bring all our needs and frustrations and worries—all those things which inhibit our joy—before God.

We have such marvelous encouragements to pray in the promises of Jesus:

"Ask, and it will be given you; seek, and you will find; knock, and it will be opened to you" (Luke 11:9).

"If you abide in me, and my words abide in you, ask whatever you will, and it shall be done for you" (John 15:7).

"Whatever you ask in prayer, you will receive, if you have faith" (Matt. 21:22).

"Whatever you ask in my name, I will do it, that the Father may be glorified in the Son" (John 14:13).

"Whatever you ask in prayer, believe that you receive it, and you will" (Mark 11:24).

In view of promises like these, why do we make so little use of this great gift? The excuse that comes to mind most quickly is, "Well, I just don't seem to have enough time." Yet it is often true—though painful to admit—that we have enough time for what we consider to be really important. If we spend time in front of the TV or reading a novel or washing the car, or even in doing church work—if we do these things instead of praying, it is because we really consider these activities to be more important.

But there is another, more serious reason why we so easily turn to the TV or some light reading at the end of a day's work: prayer—except for rare moments—is often hard work, and the results may not always be dramatically visible. As great a believer as Leslie Weatherhead admitted, "I have always found prayer difficult. So often it seems like a fruitless game of hide and seek in which we seek and God hides. I know God is very patient with me. Without that patience I should be lost. But frankly, I have to be patient with him. With no other friend would I go on seeking with such scant conscious response. Yet I cannot leave prayer alone for long. My need drives me to him. And I have a feeling that he has his own reasons for hiding himself, and that finally all my seeking will prove infinitely worthwhile."

So even when the promises of God fail to motivate us, we may be driven to pray by our own needs or the needs of those we love. And if even these do not move us, we have a final reason to pray, and it is the most basic of all: God has commanded us to pray. Therefore, prayer is not optional for us, something for us to do when we are in the mood, and it is not an activity reserved for especially religious people. And so we ought to pray—not because it makes us feel good, not because of our needs only, not because of the great promises—but finally because it is God's will that we do so. And if we pray in simple obedience, the joy that Christ promised will be ours.

Some find it natural to pray for all the little things of life, the daily decisions, the routine tasks, the immediate needs. And God is concerned with these. Nothing is too petty to bring before him who taught us to pray, "Give us today our daily bread."

If we are to have a complete prayer life, we will not stop with our immediate problems. We will bring before God the big questions of life: "Who am I? What is life all about? What am I to do with my life? How am I to relate to the people around me?" We need answers to these questions if we are to live a life of joy.

While it is natural that our prayers begin with our own needs and problems, our prayers should spread out like ripples from a pebble thrown into a pond. We begin with those closest to us, family and friends, asking that God's will be done in their lives. Dietrich Bonhoeffer wrote: "From the moment we awake until we fall asleep we must commend our loved ones wholly and unreservedly to God and leave them in his hands, transforming our anxiety for them into prayers on their behalf."

And then let us in a similar way take all the troubles of the world, the needs of the hungry, the oppressed, the sick, the imprisoned, and bring them before God, offering ourselves as sources of help. Then we can commit these problems to God and, doing so, know the joy of the man who prayed each evening, "Lord, I've been running this world all day. Now you take over."

So, putting aside our busy-ness, our doubts about prayer, and our own laziness, and mustering what faith we have, let us go on to pray, whether we feel like it or not. Then we will begin to experience that promise of Jesus, "Ask, and you will receive, that your joy may be full."

I ask, and I receive, and my joy is full.

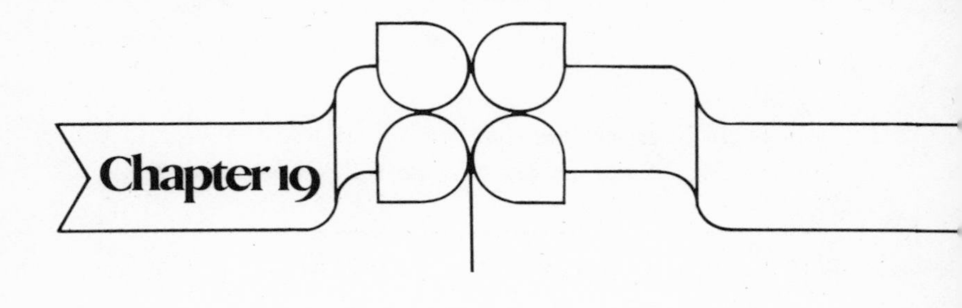

Joy in Victory

Then my head will be exalted
above the enemies who surround me;
at his tabernacle will I sacrifice with shouts of joy;
I will sing and make music to the Lord.

Psalm 27:6 NIV

A conquering army marches into the enemy stronghold, exulting in joy, the joy of victory. God wants you too to know this kind of joy—victory over your enemies.

Do you believe this? Or do you for some reason hang on to the idea that somehow God really wants you to be helpless, dejected, pitiable, depressed? God is our Father, and what father does not want the best for his children?

Who or what are the enemies over which God will give you victory? It may be a person or a group—I think especially of Christians currently being persecuted for their faith. But you may not have this kind of enemy. Your enemies may be evil forces like depression, guilt, resentment, despair, irritability, meaninglessness, fatigue—the great enemies of the spirit and destroyers of joy. Paul describes these evil forces in these words: "For we are not contending against flesh and blood, but against the principalities, against the powers, against the world rulers of this present darkness, against the spiritual hosts of wickedness in the heavenly places" (Eph. 6:12). However we understand these "principalities and powers," it is clear that we are often up against forces which are too strong for us, forces which threaten to demoralize and overwhelm us and bring us to despair. And so we pray, "Deliver us from evil."

God's good news is that we can experience victory over these forces of evil, as countless Christians have learned through the ages. If this is not yet your experience, what can you do?

1. Realize the foundation for the victory. Christ won the battle at Calvary; he conquered through his cross and resurrection. The decisive battle in the war against evil has already been fought. We still are harassed by the forces of evil, but we are fighting on the winning side. As Martin Luther wrote in his great victory hymn "A Mighty Fortress," "for us fights the valiant one, whom God himself elected."

This means we are living in a battle zone. That idea may not please us. We would prefer the comfort of a peaceful valley. If you're like me, you'd rather be Ferdinand the Bull, sitting under a cork tree, sniffing flowers, not fighting. But we really have no choice. For we are in the battle, and we must fight the good fight of faith and lay hold on eternal life, trusting in God's great Captain who fights for us.

2. Know the enemy. Before a crucial football game, a coach may send scouts ahead to observe the opposing team, trying to spot its weaknesses. In more deadly fashion, nations spy with people and planes and satellites in order to know the enemy. We can be alert to the wiles of our spiritual Enemy as we study Scripture, read books like C. S. Lewis' *Screwtape Letters,* and observe our own lives.

3. Believe that God is stronger than the enemy now. The victory of God is not just a historical occurrence, something recorded in the pages of the Bible. It is that, but if it is no more than ancient history to you, you have not yet experienced the joy of victory in your own life. God who dwells above is also with you and in you to give you victory in the present—and with that victory, joy.

4. Know your weapons. After he warns us of our spiritual enemies, Paul lists our weapons in Ephesians 6. He says, "Therefore take the whole armor of God, that you may be able to withstand in the evil day, and having done all, to stand. Stand therefore, having girded your loins with truth, and having put on the breastplate of righteousness, and having shod your feet with the equipment of the gospel of peace; besides all these, taking the shield of faith, with which you can quench all the flaming darts of the evil one. And take the helmet of salvation, and the sword of the Spirit, which is the word of God" (vv. 13-17).

Let us look briefly at each piece of our spiritual equipment:

We must know the *truth* about God, ourselves, and the enemy.

Through the gospel we receive *righteousness;* we are placed in right relationship with God, with other people, and with ourselves.

We are at *peace* when we are freed from anxiety, knowing God is with us and for us.

Faith is the shield that protects us from the fiery darts of discouragement, guilt, self-doubt, fears.

Salvation has been won for us by the life, death, and resurrection of Jesus.

Our offensive weapon is *God's Word.* As we study it and learn to use it by repeating the great promises of God, we can put to rout the forces of evil.

5. Be prepared to wait. In this age of "instant everything," we may wish for instant victory over habits of mind that have been developing for years. We need to remind ourselves of the words of Psalm 27: "Wait for the Lord; be strong, and let your heart take courage; yea, wait for the Lord!" (v. 14).

We can do this with the confidence expressed by Basilea Schlink: "Because the Victor over all sins and powers of the enemy is fighting on our side, the final victory will definitely be ours no matter how long the battle may last. There may be a long series of lost battles, but there will never be a lost war, so long as we endure in faith."

I rejoice because God is giving me victory.

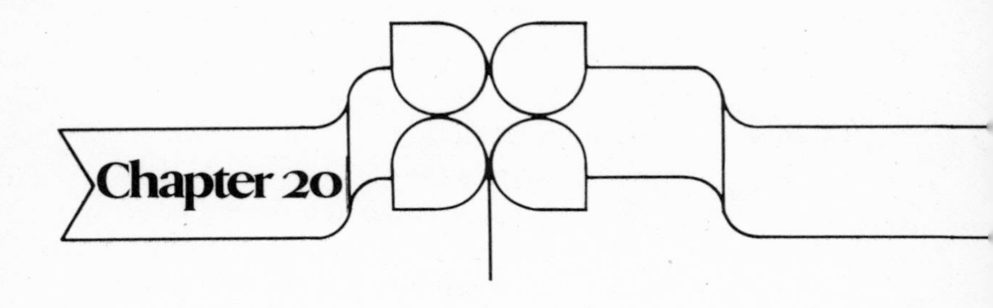

Joy Because God Rules

Clap your hands, all you nations;
shout to God with cries of joy.
How awesome is the Lord Most High,
the great King over all the earth!

Psalm 47:1-2 NIV

The headlines scream at us, and the TV and radio bombard us with bad news. Famine. Earthquakes. Mass murder. Pollution. Airline crashes. Crime. Corruption. How can we live with joy in the face of such a world?

It is possible—almost—to close one's eyes to all the misery, to shut off the TV, to cancel the newspaper, to refuse to look at *Time* or *Newsweek*. We can concentrate on our own happiness and that of our family. We can think only of our own home, our own yard, our own children, our own budget, and ignore the rest of the world.

But that is not the way of Christ. In the midst of suffering, oppressed humanity, he went about doing good. It is true that he needed time to be alone with his Father and often spent the whole night in prayer. But then he returned to face the problems, to feed the hungry, to heal the sick, to comfort the distressed.

We are called to follow him, and, if we do, we will hear from him the gracious commendation: "Come, O blessed of my Father, inherit the kingdom prepared for you from the foundation of the world; for I was hungry and you gave me food, I was thirsty and you gave me drink, I was a stranger and you welcomed me, I was naked and you clothed me, I was sick and you visited me, I was in prison and you came to me. . . . As you did it to one of the least of these my brethren, you did it to me" (Matt. 25:34-36, 40).

If we do not ignore the problems of the human family, then how do we face them without being overwhelmed by the mass of misery and our own feelings of helplessness in the face of problems which seem to have no solution?

The psalm writers answer: "The Lord reigns, let the earth be glad" (Ps. 97:1 NIV). "May the nations be glad and sing for joy, for you rule the peoples justly and guide the nations of the earth" (Ps. 67:4 NIV). "Clap your hands, all you nations; shout to God with cries of joy. How awesome is the Lord Most High, the great King over all the earth!" (Psalm 47:1-2 NIV).

The Bible teaches us that God is the ruler. He is in control. He is in charge of the world. But we have only to look around to see that at this time God's rule is not acknowledged by all. In his kingdom are rebel forces engaged against the good rule of God. And from this rebellious greed and selfishness and pride comes much of the war, the starvation, the oppression.

We don't know why God doesn't simply eliminate these rebellious forces. We may be tempted to think that if we were governing the universe, we would be able to do it much better than God. Yet the continuing existence of these evil forces seems to be part of God's overall plan for redeeming humankind and bringing together in one all things in Christ Jesus. If God is almighty, as the Bible teaches, then he could put an end right now to all the troubles and evils. And some day he will do just that. Then "every knee [shall] bow, . . . and every tongue confess that Jesus Christ is Lord, to the glory of God the Father" (Phil. 2:10-11). Meanwhile we can live believing in him, not knowing why he does what he does, but trusting in his gracious rule.

We know that the forces of evil may prosper for a time, but evil creates its own undoing and ultimately is destroyed. The Hitlers and Stalins and Idi Amins may spread terror for a time, but God is in charge, and their judgment is sure. As the poet James Russell Lowell wrote:

> Truth forever on the scaffold,
> Wrong forever on the throne,—
> Yet that scaffold sways the future,
> And, behind the dim unknown,
> Standeth God within the shadow,
> Keeping watch above his own.

One day, during the time Abraham Lincoln was president, his little son came to see him with his shirt torn and his face bleeding after a boyish fight. Lincoln was in his office in the White House. The boy approached one of the cabinet members, who said with a condescending smile, "Oh, do you want to see the president of the United States?" The little boy replied, "No, I want to see my father."

So we can live with the faith that the God who rules is also our Father. We can confess, "I believe in God the Father . . . ." And we can pray, "Our Father in heaven . . ." and, "Your kingdom come. . . . for the kingdom, the power, and the glory are yours, now and forever." And one day we will be among the jubilant victors who will cry before the throne of God, "Hallelujah! for the Lord God omnipotent reigneth."

I rejoice because God rules.

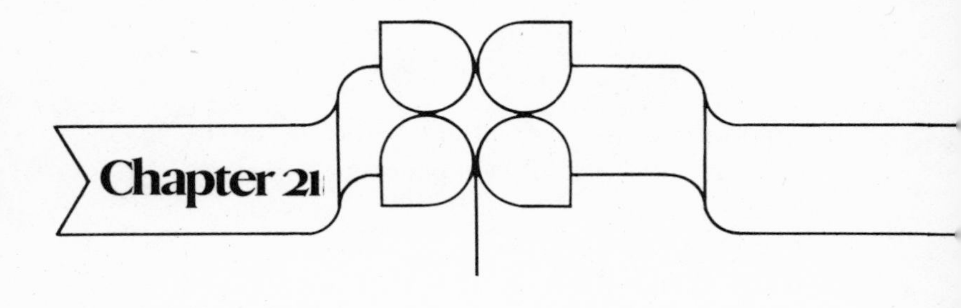

Joy in Work

For you make me glad by your deeds, O Lord;
I sing for joy at the works of your hands.

Psalm 92:4 NIV

Do we think of God as someone who works or as someone sitting high on a cloud remotely watching over his creation? Jesus said, "My Father is working still, and I am working" (John 5:17). We have a God who works for us.

When we consider God's work, we may think first of his creation of the universe. He is the God who made all things. But God's work is not past tense. He did not just make a world, like some clockmaker, and wind it up and leave it alone. His creative energy continues to hold the universe together. He is at work in every new sunrise, every growing plant, each new birth. We can see the earth constantly renewed and restored by the continuing work of God.

We can see God's work in all the agencies of life that help to feed, clothe, heal, and educate us, and to create justice.

Wherever there is a movement toward life and wholeness, there is God at work. This work of God, as we contemplate it, can evoke in us the reaction of the psalmist: "For you make me glad by your deeds, O Lord; I sing for joy at the works of your hands."

St. Paul said, "Work out your own salvation with fear and trembling; for God is at work in you, both to will and to work for his good pleasure" (Phil. 2:12). We work because God works in us and through us. By the work we do we share in the work of God today. And this work is meant to be one of our greatest sources of joy. W. R. Inge has said, "To do our duty in our own sphere, to try to create something worth creating, as our life's work, is the way to understand what joy is in this life." The Swiss doctor Paul Tournier wrote, "A conviction of vocation—any vocation—is a real motive force in a person's life, ensuring full physical development, psychic equilibrium, and spiritual joy." This means that joy does not come only from ease, or from passive entertainment, but from active work.

Because we want to be realistic about joy, we should recognize that not all work is always joyful. Much work is plainly in itself tedious: routine household tasks, stacks of test papers to be corrected, repetitive work on an assembly line, endless typing and filing in an office.

Is there any way for these types of routine work to be made joyful? One answer is no. Not all of life can be made joyful; that is an unrealistic expectation. We may as well stop fretting about it and find ways of doing the routine work as efficiently as we can and with as little resentment as we can manage.

But another answer is yes, even in these little tasks we can find joy—if they are done consistently as part of the work God is doing through us, if we do them in love for him and for one another. Bernard Ramm says, "Jesus Christ can put joy into the joyless work of the twentieth century."

Yet no matter how well we manage the routine tasks that we do from a sense of duty, it is important for each of us to discover some work in which we find true joy, even if we can do it for only a few hours a week. Ask yourself: What work gives me joy? Your answer to that question gives you a clue as to what God wants you to do in life. For if you are working at your true vocation, I believe you will find joy in it. In her book *Eighth Day of Creation* Elizabeth O'Connor says: "We ask to know the will of God without guessing that his will is written into our very beings. We perceive that will when we discern our gifts. Our obedience and surrender to God are in large part our obedience and surrender to our gifts."

Anne Morrow Lindbergh says in *Gift from the Sea,* "Nothing feeds the Center so much as creative work." I think that is because we all are made in the image of God the creator, and therefore we are all made to create. This does not mean that all of us must become painters or poets. Creative work may be decorating a home, planning a menu, designing a new machine, sewing clothes, building furniture, or finding new ways of relating to friends or family.

These creative tasks may not always be easy. They may involve the risk of failure. They may involve some routine, detailed work. But when we do creative work like this, we are following in the footsteps of our Father, who is the Creator and who still recreates his world.

In a culture like ours that emphasizes entertainment and leisure, those of us who are parents or teachers may bless our children by teaching them a positive attitude toward work. The American industrialist Henry J. Kaiser was taught this lesson by his mother, who worked hard as a volunteer nurse. She told him, "Henry, nothing is ever accomplished without

work. If I leave you nothing else but the will to work, I will have left you the priceless gift: the joy of work."

I rejoice in my work knowing God is at work in me.

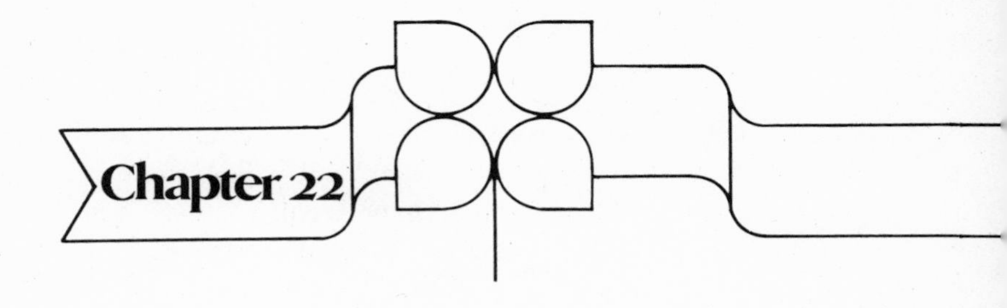

The Joy of the Lord Is Your Strength

The joy of the Lord is your strength.

Nehemiah 8:10

It was about 400 years before the birth of Jesus. The Jewish people had undergone a great chastening. They had forsaken the worship of the true God and turned to idols. Corruption, greed, and selfishness had taken the place of a united people caring for one another. Then Babylon, a powerful city-state from the east, had conquered them and led them into captivity.

For nearly 70 years the Jewish people lived as exiles, slaves in a foreign land. But they did not lose hope. God's messengers, the prophets, kept alive the hope that one day they would return to their promised land.

Finally, under the leadership of Ezra and Nehemiah, they did return to rebuild their ravaged country. In the course of their rebuilding they discovered the book of the law, God's Word to them, and Ezra and Nehemiah gathered the people and read to them.

When the law was read and interpreted, the people broke

into weeping: tears of repentance, tears over the mistakes of the past, tears over all the lost dreams and hopes. Then the people were told, "Do not mourn or weep. . . . Go your way, eat the fat and drink sweet wine and send portions to him for whom nothing is prepared; for this day is holy to our Lord; and do not be grieved, for the joy of the Lord is your strength."

There is a proper time for the tears of repentance, but the people were not to wallow in their regrets over the past. They were to celebrate God's gifts in the present, and to share with those who lacked. There is a time to let go of the past and its missed opportunities, a time to celebrate present joy.

The apostle Paul could have been consumed by regrets about the past. He could have wallowed in guilt as he remembered his cooperation in the stoning of Stephen and his persecution of Christians. He could have wallowed in self-pity as he remembered the beatings, stonings, shipwrecks, the rejection he had suffered. Instead he said, "One thing I do, forgetting what lies behind and straining forward to what lies ahead, I press on toward the goal for the prize of the upward call of God in Christ Jesus" (Phil. 3:13-14).

A person depressed over regrets about the past, over sins and missed opportunities and shortcomings, is in danger. Depression leads to weakness of spirit, mind, and body. Conversely, the person filled with joy is strong in spirit, mind, and body. "The joy of the Lord is your strength."

I find that when I'm depressed, I am more subject to temptations of all kinds: the temptation to be critical of others, the temptation to self-pity, the temptation to overeat. But when I am experiencing joy, I am more able to withstand the temptations, or they do not even tempt me.

As doctors so often emphasize today, there is a close connection between our bodies and our minds and spirits. Medical personnel find a close relationship between personality and major health problems. When we are depressed or dejected, the toll is taken in our cells and tissues and organs. Even for the sake of our own bodies we should desire to be as joyful as possible. Martin Luther said, "I should be so joyful that I ought to be entirely well for joy, and for very joy it ought to be impossible for me to become sick."

A contemporary pastor writes, "So many of us spend most of our time brooding over the troubles of the past, grumbling about the present, and worrying about the future. All these follies are destructive and leave no room for health, peace, love, and joy."

When we are filled with regret over sins of the past, we can set our minds on promises like these: "If our conscience condemns us, we know that God is greater than our conscience" (1 John 3:20 TEV) and "If we confess our sins, he is faithful and just, and will forgive our sins and cleanse us from all unrighteousness" (1 John 1:9).

Then we can go on to look to this day, to rejoice in the Lord in this present moment, to say, "This is the day the Lord has made; let us rejoice and be glad in it" (Ps. 118:24 NIV).

In her book *Either Way I Win,* Lois Johnson tells of her struggle with cancer and the lessons she learned about prayer. She writes: "Because of prayer support, I was able to offer praise during my hospitalization and in the weeks immediately following. Often I fell asleep praying, 'Thank you, Jesus. Alleluia,' or 'I praise you, Lord.' Not thank you *for* evil, but thanks for bringing good, even out of cancer. Many people continued to pray daily, and their intercessions carried me through the time when I had to learn the discipline of praise. If unable to say the words, I sang old hymns or new choruses of adoration. Out of that obedience, I lived the meaning of Nehemiah 8:10: '. . . the joy of the Lord is your strength.' "

The joy of the Lord is my strength.

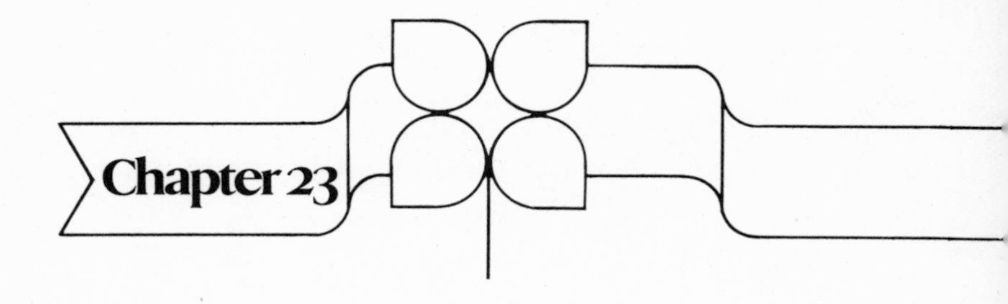

The Joy of Fellowship

As I remember your tears, I long night and day to see you, that I may be filled with joy.

2 Timothy 1:4

Time and again Paul sang the joys of Christian fellowship. To the Christians at Rome he wrote, stating his hope "that by God's will I may come to you with joy and be refreshed in your company" (Rom. 15:32). To the Philippians he wrote, "I thank my God in all my remembrance of you, always in every prayer of mine for you all making my prayer with joy, thankful for your partnership in the gospel from the first day until now" (Phil. 1:3-5). To his young co-worker Timothy he exclaimed, "I long night and day to see you, that I may be filled with joy" (2 Tim. 1:4). When Paul sent the runaway slave Onesimus back to his owner Philemon, he said, "I have derived much joy and comfort from your love, my brother, because the hearts of the saints have been refreshed through you" (Philemon 7).

The joy of true Christian fellowship means much more than membership in the same church. It is a meeting in Christ to share the things of the Spirit. That does not mean that we spend all our time talking "religion," but that our relationship to Christ informs all our conversation. When true Christian fellowship happens, it sweeps away barriers of age, of sex, of denomination, of social background as hearts and minds touch in shared faith and shared experience. We may enjoy such moments only rarely, but when they come they are a great gift of God.

Paul's longing for fellowship is the longing felt by many other Christian missionaries since his time. When our family lived in an isolated corner of Madagascar, one of our greatest longings was for the fellowship of certain friends in the Lord. We could echo Paul's words, "I long night and day to see you, that I may be filled with joy." One of the greatest hardships missionaries face is the isolation from family and friends. They may be the only Christians in their area, or, if there are local Christians, fellowship may be limited by language and cultural barriers. Today the missionary is no longer seen as a conquering hero and may often be serving under a hostile government or under local church leaders struggling to be free of outside domination. In the midst of strains like these, missionaries need all the fellowship they can find, and Christians "back home" can offer this through letters or the sharing of a magazine, a good book, or an inspiring tape. And missionaries will always find joy in knowing you are praying for them.

It is a rare Christian who never experiences the joys of fellowship, but it is even more rare to find one who has enough. Nearly all of us feel the need and the desire for the joy of true and deep Christian fellowship. How can we open ourselves to receive more of this gift?

1. Admit that we need one another. This may be hard, especially if you have been taught that you should stand on your own two feet, that it is a sign of weakness to need someone else. I remember when a friend came to me and said, "For the past two months I've been so depressed that I was considering killing myself, and many times I thought of coming to talk to you, but I didn't want to admit that I couldn't make it by myself." We do need one another, we are meant for one another, and, as part of the body of Christ, we are not expected to go it alone. We need one another, and we should not be ashamed of that.

2. *Pray for fellowship.* As in so many other areas of our lives, the sad words are true: "You do not have, because you do not ask" (James 4:2). Persist in prayer until God in his own good timing gives you the fellowship you need.

3. *Run the risk of openness.* There may be others in your neighborhood, your place of work, or your church who are just as eager as you for Christian fellowship. You may have to risk being laughed at, or being considered a religious fanatic, or a weak person. Even with members of your own church you may have to run the risk of rejection if you begin to discuss your own needs or doubts or questions. But without the risk you may never find the fellowship you seek. The other person may be there just waiting for you to take the first step.

4. *Be ready to invest the time needed to sustain a deep friendship.* A relationship that gets beyond the surface and stays there requires a greater investment of time than one based on superficial chatter. But the rewards are equally great. If Christian fellowship is important to you, then arrange your time to provide for it. Take time to visit a friend, to read and study together; set aside time to write a letter, to make a phone call. As the depth of your friendship grows, so will the joys.

5. *Support your fellowship with prayer.* Our relationship can grow even in physical absence if we share our joys and

problems in prayer. Warren Wiersbe, pastor of Moody Church in Chicago, has said, "Perhaps the deepest Christian fellowship and joy we can experience in this life is at the throne of Grace, praying with and for one another."

I have the joy of fellowship.

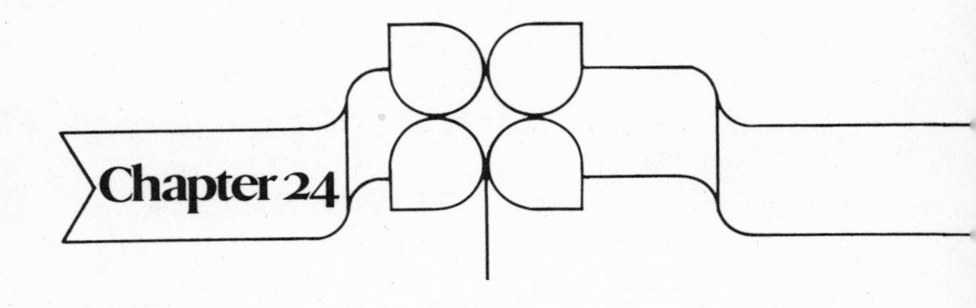

Joy in Growing

I know that I shall remain and continue with you all, for your progress and joy in the faith, so that in me you may have ample cause to glory in Christ Jesus, because of my coming to you again.

Philippians 1:25-26

Paul's letter to the Philippians has been called "The Epistle of Joy." In it the verb *rejoice* occurs eleven times, and the noun *joy* appears five times. This is all the more surprising because the letter was written from prison by a man facing the possibility of imminent death.

The prospect of execution leaves Paul feeling ambivalent. On the one hand, Christ means so much to him that he longs to be fully with him. On the other hand, he also wants to help the Philippian Christians to grow in the faith. He writes to them: "I am pulled in two directions. I want very much to leave this life and be with Christ, which is a far better thing; but for your sake it is much more important that I remain alive. I am sure of this, and so I know that I will stay. I will stay on with you all, to add to your progress and joy in the faith" (Phil. 1:23-25 TEV).

Paul here links joy with progress in the faith. And Peter writes, "Grow in the grace and knowledge of our Lord and Savior Jesus Christ" (2 Peter 3:18). One of the ways we experience joy in our lives is through progress or growth.

I believe that one of the most natural feelings in the world is the desire to grow. We are made for growth, not for stagnation. I know that when I am not growing, when I am bogged down, then the joy seeps out of my life and I feel lost and depressed. I need the challenge of growth, of creativity, of reaching for the next goal. When I am faithful to the talents God has given me, when I work each day to develop and improve them, I find joy.

As Christians we can never be satisfied with having arrived. If you are not experiencing the fulness of God's joy in your life, you might ask yourself: Am I still growing in the faith? If not, what can I do to begin again? Today we are blessed with so many opportunities for growth through books, classes, discussion groups, tapes, correspondence courses, retreats, and conferences that no one need be denied the opportunity to grow in the faith.

We find joy when we grow, and we find joy when we help others grow. Paul looked forward to visiting the Philippians for *their* progress and joy in the faith. To the Christians at Thessalonica he wrote: "For what is our hope or joy or crown of boasting before our Lord Jesus Christ at his coming? Is it not for you? For you are our glory and joy" (1 Thess. 2:19-20). When Paul thinks of Jesus' coming again, he imagines that his joy at that time will include his joy in seeing these Christians in heaven. They will be there because through Paul's teaching the Holy Spirit brought them to faith. Paul says farther on in the same letter: "For what thanksgiving can we render to God for you, for all the joy which we feel for your sake before our God, praying earnestly day and night that we may see you face to face and supply what is lacking in your faith?" (3:9-10).

I have been a teacher on and off in various situations for nearly 20 years, and, as any teacher can testify, what keeps a teacher going in the midst of disappointments or frustrations is the joy that comes from the student who does learn—who learns to read or write with greater understanding, whose mind catches fire with a new idea, or whose faith comes alive through our teaching.

The apostle John, writing to some of his spiritual children, said, "No greater joy can I have than this, to hear that my children follow the truth" (3 John 4). This can be said by any faithful teacher or parent. Here is especially a word of joy for parents today who face the frightening, but still joyful prospect of raising Christian children. Many people are choosing not to have children so that they can have greater freedom and material benefits. Still others have downplayed the role of housewife and mother so that sometimes those women who are committed to staying home and teaching their own children and providing good homes for their husbands are made to feel guilty or inferior because they do not have an outside "career."

Yet in the midst of the daily tasks of caring for a family and the difficulties of helping children grow, the faithful mother and wife has many moments of joy. She can also look forward to the joy of seeing children leading happy, fulfilled, godly lives. "No greater joy can I have than this, to hear that my children follow the truth."

As our heavenly Father, God finds the same joy in us. Catherine Marshall writes, "What He wants for us is exactly what every thoughtful parent wants for his child—that pure, deep-flowing joy that springs out of maturity and fulfillment."

I rejoice as I grow and help others grow.

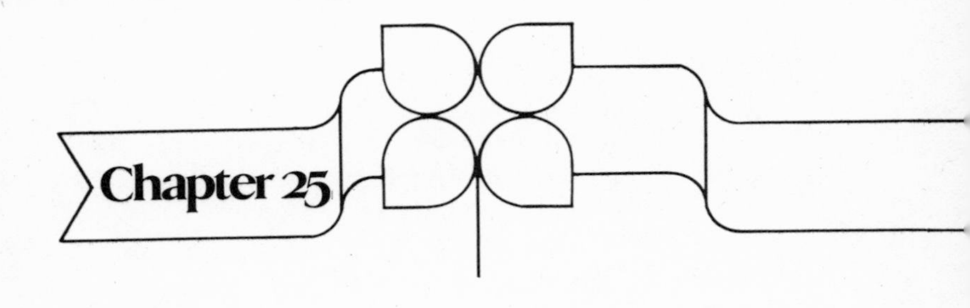

Joy in Refuge

Let all who take refuge in you be glad;
let them ever sing for joy.
Spread your protection over them;
that those who love your name may rejoice in you.

Psalm 5:11 NIV

Ours has been an age of refugees. We have seen so many pictures of ragged, tired, frightened people, trudging with their few pitiable possessions, escaping in rafts or small boats, struggling through the jungle, or escaping across armed frontiers. When we see them, we feel pity and terror. And we feel relief and we share in their joy when they find refuge in a friendly country.

There are times when we too become refugees, when we flee before the onslaughts of life, when we are exhausted in mind and heart. Then we can know the quiet joy of finding refuge in God, like a tired and tear-stained child creeping into the arms of mother or father. When we seek refuge in God, we will know the joy that comes from his comfort.

Robert C. Frost, in his book *Overflowing Life,* speaks of a spiritual law of opposites: "The heavenly streams of the Spirit spring forth most vigorously from the earthly ground of contrasting circumstances. It is in restless times that we discover His rest; in turmoil, that we find peace; in irritation, that we find patience; in resentment, that we perfect forgiveness; and in distress, that we experience joy."

When our son Paul was three or four years old, he would sometimes awaken in the middle of the night, terrified, I suppose, by bad dreams. Sometimes I would lie down on the floor next to his bed, and he would be calmed and go back to sleep. The frightening darkness was still there, but he knew I was there in the darkness beside him.

When the darkness of life and its problems descend on us, we may wish we could still curl up in someone's lap and be safe and secure. We can find refuge when we turn to God in trust and prayer. The psalmist encourages us, "Let all who take refuge in you be glad; let them ever sing for joy."

One Christian who found joy in suffering by seeking refuge in God was Edith Reuss, a young wife and mother who died of lupus at age 34. Before her death she wrote, "Joy is knowing that even our crosses in life can be used by God for his glory and our good. We are too finite to see the overall picture, but we can trustingly thank him even for the pain in life because we have the assurance that though he doesn't deliberately cause us pain, he is still there and in control. Joy is this reassurance, but it is also more.

"Joy is a deep soul-releasing knowledge that whatever our situation, God is hanging in there with us. He rejoices when we rejoice; he cries when we cry. He allows us our free will even though he knows we will hurt ourselves by it, just because he loves us so much. He is always there. Emmanuel, God with us. As far as I know, this is ultimate joy. It is something that death and depression, doubt and lupus flares cannot weaken. Is there even more joy than this? I wonder and thrill at the possibilities."

Particularly at those times when our faith is weak, when we may doubt that he is there, we need to seek refuge in God. We can do this, not by our emotions because they may be all wrong, but by a simple act of will. We can turn to him, look to him, speak to him. George Macdonald wrote: "That man is perfect in faith who can come to God in the utter dearth of his feelings and desires, without a glow or an aspiration, with the weight of low thoughts, failures, neglects, and wandering forgetfulness, and say to Him, 'Thou art my refuge.' "

At these times it may help us to repeat over and over Bible verses like these:

"God is our refuge and strength, a present help in trouble" (Ps. 46:1).

"Come to me, all who labor and are heavy laden, and I will give you rest" (Matt. 11:28).

"Lo, I am with you always, to the close of the age" (Matt. 28:20).

Or to build our faith, we can say personal statements of truth like these:

"God is with me now and always."

"God is my refuge and strength."

"I am a child of God; God loves me."

We can repeat these Bible verses or statements of faith when we awake, or before sleeping, or many times during the day. As we do so, these spiritual truths slip deep into our subconscious minds to comfort and strengthen us and to increase our joy.

I take refuge in God and rejoice.

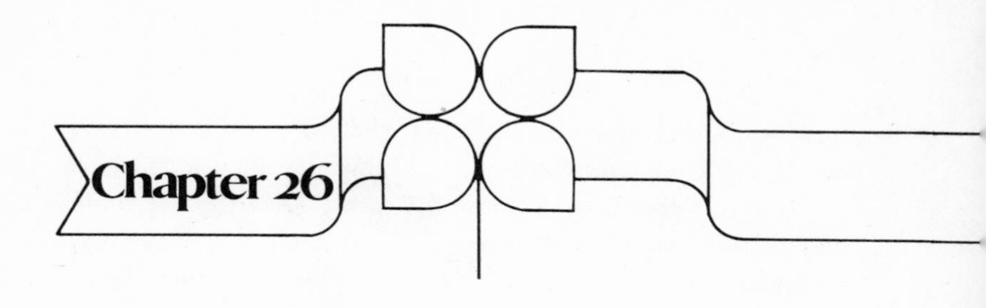

Joy After Weeping

Truly, truly, I say to you, you will weep and lament, but the world will rejoice; you will be sorrowful, but your sorrow will turn into joy.

John 16:20

On the evening before his crucifixion Jesus told his disciples, "A little while, and you will see me no more; again a little while, and you will see me" (John 16:16). They were dismayed by these words. How could they get along without him? How could they live in the absence of the One who gave their lives meaning and purpose? What lay before them were only tears of separation.

But Jesus went on to say, "Your sorrow will turn into joy. When a woman is in travail she has sorrow, because her hour has come; but when she is delivered of the child, she no longer remembers the anguish, for joy that a child is born into the world. So you have sorrow now, but I will see you again and your hearts will rejoice, and no one will take your joy from you" (vv. 20-22).

These words took on special meaning for me when our first

child was born. My wife endured 34 hours of difficult labor and then a caesarean section. All through that long, long night I was thinking, *"That's the last time we go through this. Never again!"* But within a day after the birth of our daughter, my wife was talking about having another baby. "She no longer remembers the anguish, for joy that a child is born into the world."

We have in this passage another example of the realistic joy of the Bible. It does not say that our lives will be 100 percent pure joy. It says, "You will weep and lament," "you will be sorrowful," "you have sorrow now." Our lives will contain sorrow; that is the nature of this present life. But the great point is this: the sorrow is temporary, the joy is permanent. "No one will take your joy from you."

We live in a time when there is much sorrow in the world because of wars, earthquakes, disease, famine. But the Bible points us to another time, a time when these sorrows will end and when God's perfect rule will be established. The book of Revelation gives us a glorious picture of the people of God, cleansed by the blood of the Lamb, arrayed in white robes, their sorrow turned to joy: "Therefore are they before the throne of God, and serve him day and night within his temple; and he who sits upon the throne will shelter them with his presence. They shall hunger no more, neither thirst any more; the sun shall not strike them, nor any scorching heat. For the Lamb in the midst of the throne will be their shepherd, and he will guide them to springs of living water; and God will wipe away every tear from their eyes" (Rev. 7:15-17).

We too may be called upon to suffer the sorrow of separation from loved ones, the sorrow of watching others suffer, the sorrow of failed plans. If we admit the sorrow, accept it, and express it with tears, we will open the way to joy much sooner than if we bottle up the sorrow within us.

Here most women in our society are wiser than men, who have been taught that it is wrong—or at least a sign of weakness—to cry. We men sometimes forget that at the grave of his friend Lazarus, Jesus wept. The tears of sorrow make it possible for the joy to break through. Psalm 126 declares: "May those who sow in tears reap with shouts of joy! He that goes forth weeping, bearing the seed for sowing, shall come home with shouts of joy, bringing his sheaves with him" (vv. 5-6).

Many of earth's joys are preceded by a time of sorrow, a time of preparation. The "sorrow" may be as simple as the sore back and blistered hands that a backyard gardener experiences in spring. Or it may be the anxieties of childrearing, when parents struggle to cope with all the problems of teenagers, with the feelings of inadequacy, with fears for the future. The musician who wants the joy of mastering an instrument must put in long hours of arduous practice. If we shun the hard work of planting seeds, we will never experience the joy of the harvest.

Some sorrows are brief. But sorrow becomes almost unbearable if we think it will last forever, when sorrow seems to stretch before us like a hall of mirrors, sorrow reflecting sorrow. Fortunately for us, there is the blessed trick of memory whereby we tend to remember the good and forget much of the pain. Yet at the time we are experiencing sorrow, that's hard to remember. And some sorrows, like the loss of a loved one, will never be completely erased. Some measure of sorrow will remain as long as the separation endures. Yet the Christian hope is that even this separation will not be permanent. A joyful reunion awaits us. "Weeping may tarry for the night, but joy comes with the morning" (Ps. 30:5).

My sorrow will be turned into joy.

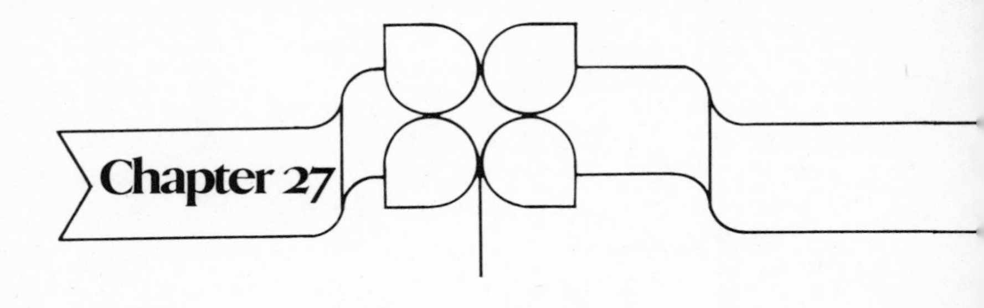

Joy Shared

Rejoice with those who rejoice.

Romans 12:15

Mark Twain said, "Grief can take care of itself; but to get the full value of joy, you must have somebody to share it with." James M. Barrie wrote, "Those who bring sunshine to the lives of others cannot keep it from themselves." And Paul urges us to "Rejoice with those who rejoice."

The famous literacy pioneer, Frank Laubach, wrote a book called *Channels of Spiritual Power*. In it he speaks of Christians as channels with one end open to God and the other open to the people around us. If both ends remain open, the love and power and peace and joy of God flow through us—from God to the people around us.

It is possible for this channel to become blocked up. If I neglect prayer and God's Word, my channel is blocked toward God. But if I turn away from those around me, this also blocks the flow. God can give me no more until I share what I have.

We can use this picture in our thoughts about joy. If I do

not have God's joy flowing through me, it may be that I have not been open to God. In that case, I need to take time to turn to him in faithful prayer, to meditate on his Word, to open myself to the influence of the Holy Spirit.

If we are convinced that we have been open to God, but we still do not feel the flow of joy through us, we can test whether we are sharing joy with others. As I give joy to others, I am open to receive joy from God. There's a little song that says, "Love is something if you give it away, you end up having more." We could change that to say, "Joy is something if you give it away, you end up having more."

If I want more joy in my life, I can think of the ways each day I can bring joy to others—by a friendly smile, a helping hand, a timely phone call, an appreciative letter, a bouquet of flowers, a plateful of cookies, a special meal.

Joy is not meant to be trapped within us, but to flow like a fountain from the depths of our being. It is as we express our joy, in words or actions, that we open the way for more joy to flow in us and through us.

One special way to express our joy and to share it with others is through music. The Bible repeatedly encourages us to "make a joyful noise to the Lord" (Ps. 98:4); "Let the nations be glad and sing for joy" (Ps. 67:4); "Tell of his deeds in songs of joy" (Ps. 107:22); "Let them ever sing for joy" (Ps. 5:11).

When we sing or play an instrument to express our faith, we open the way for joy to be released in us. Martin Luther once wrote to a man named Matthias Weller, who was subject to spells of depression: "There is no sacrifice lovelier and more pleasing than a cheerful heart, joyful in the Lord. Therefore when you are sad, and this spirit threatens to gain the upper hand, you should say: Come on! I must play our Lord Christ a song on the organ . . . for Scripture teaches me that

He is pleased to hear a cheerful song and the music of stringed instruments. And go at the keys with gusto, as did David and Elisha, until the heavy thoughts disappear. If the devil returns and prompts you to worry or to have sad thoughts, defend yourself bravely and say, 'Devil, get out. I must now sing and play to my Lord Christ.' "

My wife, who loves to sing, appreciates the old proverb, "He who sings prays twice." If we are singing to an audience, whether in a child's bedroom or a great concert hall, our songs bless us and bless those who hear us. And so the joy is shared, and we are built up spiritually. Paul urges us, "Be filled with the Spirit, addressing one another in psalms and hymns and spiritual songs, singing and making melody to the Lord with all your heart, always and for everything giving thanks in the name of our Lord Jesus Christ to God the Father" (Eph. 5:18-20).

Another way we can share the joy we have found in Christ is by joining with others to work toward feeding the hungry of the world, comforting the lonely and imprisoned, healing the sick in mind and body, bringing justice to the oppressed, and promoting peace in the world. By sharing with others, we can know the joy of giving.

For Christian joy is an active thing, flowing through us and out to others. E. Stanley Jones, missionary to India, said, "Christian joy is joy with its sleeves rolled up, ready to go anywhere, to do anything to help a suffering humanity and help it to sing."

I am blessed as I share my joy.

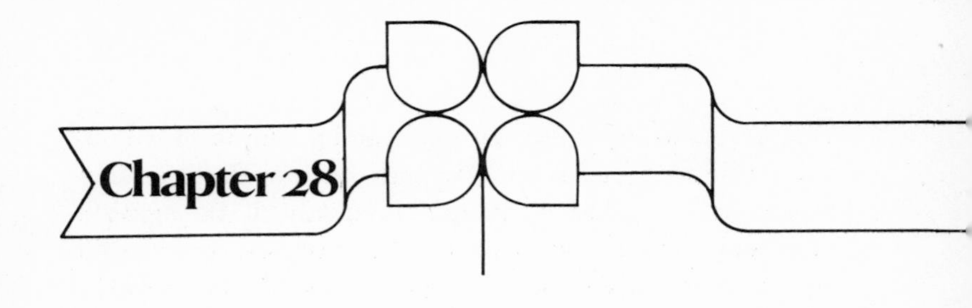

Joy in Suffering

Beloved, do not be surprised at the fiery ordeal which comes upon you to prove you, as though something strange were happening to you. But rejoice in so far as you share Christ's sufferings, that you may rejoice and be glad when his glory is revealed.

1 Peter 4:12-13

The Old Testament abounds in expressions of joy at the blessings of God. But the New Testament goes beyond this. For it speaks of the joy that comes in suffering. This is the mysterious, supernatural joy born of the Holy Spirit. This joy in suffering comes from our being identified with the Jesus who is our suffering Savior and the Jesus who will come again in glory as victorious Lord and King.

The Bible speaks of the church, the totality of Christians in the world, as the body of Christ. As part of Christ's body, our sufferings become his sufferings. The Scriptures even speak of our *completing* the suffering of Jesus. Paul writes, "And now I am happy about my sufferings for you, for by means of my physical sufferings I am helping to complete what still remains of Christ's sufferings on behalf of his body, the church" (Col. 1:24 TEV). Peter wrote to suffering Christians, "Rejoice in so far as you share Christ's sufferings." And Paul wrote to the Philippians, "For you have been given the privilege of serving Christ, not only by believing in him, but also by suffering for him" (1:29 TEV).

A contemporary example of a Christian finding meaning in suffering comes from a missionary doctor, Helen Roseveare. In her autobiography, *Give Me This Mountain,* she writes about the civil war that followed the independence of the Congo in 1963. She and other missionaries were captured by rebel forces. They were imprisoned, terrorized, locked up with little food or water. Every day for five months they faced the possibility that they would all be killed.

After her release Helen Roseveare said, "In my heart was an amazing peace, a realization that I was being highly privileged to be identified with Him in a new way, the way of Calvary. I witnessed the outpouring of hatred against the white man. I became very conscious of the extent to which we had earned this. If I was willing to be identified as a European with the sin of the white people against the African in the past fifty or more years—the injustice, the cruelties, the hardships, cheap labor with flogging, black womenfolk and illegitimate children, bribery and corruption in courts and administration—then perhaps, in some small way, I was privileged to be part of the extirpation of that sin. We whites had to be identified with it, to bear its penalty, to suffer for it, that Africa might be rid of it. This was our hope; this is what made it worthwhile."

In a similar way, we may be called on, as part of the body of Christ, to bear the suffering in certain painful situations in in our cities, our families, our nations, the world. But we can offer our sufferings to God in the hope that our suffering may change the situation, that our suffering may be the means of releasing the healing power of God.

In the book of Romans Paul writes, "Therefore, since we are justified by faith, we have peace with God through our Lord Jesus Christ. Through him we have obtained access to this grace in which we stand, and we rejoice in our hope of sharing the glory of God. More than that, we rejoice in our sufferings, knowing that suffering produces endurance, and endurance produces character, and character produces hope, and hope does not disappoint us" (5:1-5).

Here is one of those topics where we must speak soberly, especially to those who are enduring suffering. Suffering does not always build character. Some people are made stronger, wiser, more compassionate by suffering. Others find only self-pity and bitterness. So much depends on the attitude with which the suffering is accepted. We are affected not only by what happens, but by our response to what happens.

It does seem that for certain kinds of growth, suffering is a necessity. Any parent knows that before a child comes to maturity, he or she must suffer some pain, disappointment, and failure. The parent who tries to shield a child from all these hurts of life is not doing the child a favor. The pampered child is not necessarily the one best prepared to face the realities of life. In helping a child learn to walk, we have to let him fall; the good parent has to give a child enough room to make mistakes. In this process the parent does not enjoy watching the child fall or suffer, rather the parent suffers with the child. Yet with a wisdom that is greater than the child's, the parent allows the suffering that will lead to growth and maturity.

We believe that God is not only aware of our suffering, but that as our heavenly Father, he shares our pain. We are intimately linked to God in our sufferings. We share Christ's sufferings in the world, and he shares ours. It is this conviction that enables us to rejoice in the midst of our sufferings, knowing God is with us, and that beyond our sufferings is a good future secure in God.

Billy Graham has said, "Thousands of Christians have learned the secret of contentment and joy in trial. Some of the happiest Christians I have met have been life-long sufferers. They have had every reason to sigh and complain, being denied so many privileges and pleasures that they see others enjoy, yet they have found greater cause for gratitude and joy than many who are prosperous, vigorous and strong. In all ages Christians have found it possible to maintain the spirit of joy in the hour of trial. In circumstances that would have felled most men, they have so completely risen above them that they actually have used the circumstances to serve and glorify Christ."

I rejoice as I share Christ's sufferings.

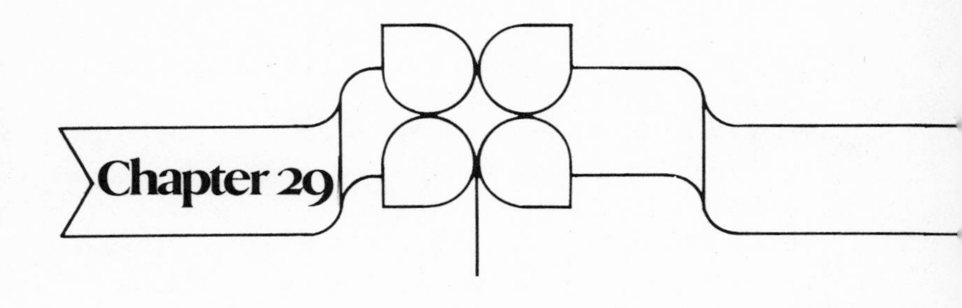

Joy in Persecution

Blessed are you when men hate you, and when they exclude you and revile you, and cast out your name as evil, on account of the Son of Man! Rejoice in that day, and leap for joy, for behold, your reward is great in heaven; for so their fathers did to the prophets.

Luke 6:22-23

Writing from prison, an early Christian said: "In a dark hole I have found cheerfulness; in a place of bitterness and death I have found rest. While others weep I have found laughter, where others fear I have found strength. Who would believe that in a state of misery I have had great pleasure, that in a lonely corner I have had glorious company, and in the hardest bonds perfect repose. All these things Jesus has granted me. He is with me, comforts me and fills me with joy."

One of the things said about the early Christians was, "These people turn the world upside down." And often the Bible's message does turn our values upside down, because it is the opposite of what people commonly believe. We think, for example, of joy coming from success, from the approval and love of others. Yet Jesus says, "Blessed are you when men hate you. . . . Rejoice in that day and leap for joy." He promised his disciples, "If they persecuted me, they will persecute you" (John 15:20). And he promised them joy in the midst of persecution.

As we read the book of Acts, the stories of the first Christians, this is exactly what we find. When the apostles were imprisoned and beaten and ordered to stop speaking in the name of Jesus, "they left the presence of the council, rejoicing that they were worthy to suffer dishonor for the name (5:41). When Paul and Barnabas were persecuted in Asia Minor and driven from Antioch, "the disciples were filled with joy and with the Holy Spirit" (13:52). In Philippi Paul and Silas made the prison ring with their prayers and hymn singing. Paul wrote to the Thessalonians: "You became imitators of us and of the Lord, for you received the word in much affliction, with joy inspired by the Holy Spirit" (1 Thess. 1:6).

Someone has said, "The trouble with Christians nowadays is that no one wants to kill them anymore." That, of course, is not true everywhere in the world. There are places where Christians are being killed for the faith. This is not the case for most of us—and we can be thankful for our religious freedom. But we can also ask whether we are spared persecution because our Christianity is such a pale imitation of the real thing, so lukewarm that it doesn't arouse persecution.

Of course, killing someone is not the only way to persecute him. There are more subtle forms: the lifted eyebrow, the supercilious sneer, the sarcastic comment, the social snubbing, the condescending smile. As a child we used to chant, "Sticks and stones may break my bones, but words will never harm me." Even then I knew that was a lie. Words can hurt a lot more than sticks and stones, and the refusal to speak may hurt even more.

Perhaps hardest to bear is the persecution that comes from those closest to us: family members who do not understand why we live by a different set of values, friends who cannot accept the fact that we choose different forms of entertainment or a different standard of living. Even within the church, where we ought to expect acceptance, we may be persecuted by those who say, "You must worship the way I worship." "You must understand spiritual truths as I understand them." "You must serve others the way I think is most helpful."

Regardless of the form that persecution takes, Jesus said, "Blessed are those who are persecuted for righteousness' sake, for theirs is the kingdom of heaven" (Matt. 5:10).

In Luke 6 Jesus suggests two reasons why we can rejoice even in the midst of persecution: first, our reward is great in heaven. In the words of the old camp song, "If you don't bear the cross, then you can't wear the crown." In this life we may suffer persecution, but he has promised that he will reward us in the life to come.

Second, Jesus points out that when we are persecuted, we are in good company. The Old Testament prophets were persecuted, killed for their faithful witness to the God of Israel. Jesus himself suffered persecution, even to death. Legend has it that of the first 12 apostles only John died a natural death. And in every land and every time there have been those who suffered because of their allegiance to Christ.

In *New Joy for Daily Living* Eric Malte says, "That faith in Christ is a gift of grace wrought in the heart by the Holy Spirit and granted by divine favor, we are ready to admit and confess. But that also suffering for the sake of Christ and His Gospel is a boon granted by God's grace we find hard to recognize. And yet we have the assurance on many pages of the

Bible that we are with God and He with us in the pain we suffer for His sake. Ours is the privilege of intimate sharing in the very heart of God also in suffering."

Even in persecution I can rejoice because God is with me.

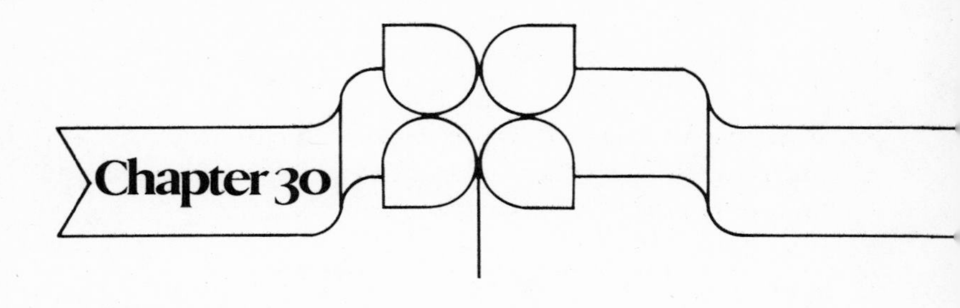

The Joy Set Before

. . . looking to Jesus the pioneer and perfecter of our faith, who for the joy that was set before him endured the cross, despising the shame, and is seated at the right hand of the throne of God.

Hebrews 12:2

In the front of a church where I would sometimes go to pray was a stained-glass window depicting Christ praying in Gethsemane, locked in prayer with his Father, facing the imminent horrors of his trial, torture, and execution, yet finally reaching the resolution, "nevertheless not my will, but thine, be done" (Luke 22:42).

Jesus could say this because he did not look only at the immediate situation, the events of the next 24 hours. With the eyes of faith he saw beyond suffering and death to the victory of the resurrection and the prospect of joyful reunion with his Father. Armed with the anticipation of that joy, he was able to endure the cross and to discount the humiliation that preceded his victory.

Matthew Henry writes: "He had something in view under all his sufferings which was pleasant to Him. He rejoiced to see by His sufferings He should make satisfaction to the injured justice of God and give security to His honor and government; that He should make peace between God and man; that He should seal the covenant of His grace, and be the mediator of it; that He should open the way of salvation to the chief of sinners, and that He should effectively save all those that the Father had given Him and Himself be the first-born among many brethren. This was the joy set before."

Hamlet, contemplating suicide, said that "the dread of something after death puzzles the will and makes us rather bear the ills we have than fly to others that we know not of." But the opposite is true for the person who sees death, not as a fearsome leap into the unknown, but as the return to a loving Father. Then the joy set before helps us bear the ills we have, not in silent resignation, but in joyful anticipation.

In some lesser ways in life we get hints of this. The joyful prospect of a vacation makes the end of the school year or the drudgery of a job more tolerable. Having the prospect of some good experience ahead of us can give strength and meaning to days in which we might otherwise falter. By keeping our eyes on the goal we can maintain our perspective and come through successfully.

I have always had a fondness for the headstrong, impetuous character of Peter. One night he and the other disciples were rowing across the Sea of Galilee. In the midst of a stormy night, the frightened disciples peered ahead into the darkness. There they saw a ghostlike figure walking on the water. Jesus, seeing their terrified reaction, called out, "Courage! It is I. Don't be afraid" (Matt. 14:27 TEV).

Typical of his character, Peter responded first, before any of the other disciples. Almost without thinking, he spoke:

"Lord, if it is really you, order me to come out on the water to you" (v. 28).

Jesus said, "Come!" and Peter stepped out of the boat in a burst of faith and began making his way to Jesus. Then Peter noticed the stormy waves; he took his eyes off Jesus; he immediately began to sink. Only the saving hand of Jesus reaching out to him rescued Peter.

Perhaps Peter learned a lesson from this, the lesson of "looking to Jesus, the pioneer and perfecter of our faith." For many years later he wrote, "Let us give thanks to the God and Father of our Lord Jesus Christ! Because of his great mercy he gave us new life by raising Jesus Christ from death. This fills us with living hope, and so we look forward to possessing the rich blessings that God keeps for his people. He keeps them for you in heaven, where they cannot decay or spoil or fade away. They are for you, who through faith are kept safe by God's power for the salvation which is ready to be revealed at the end of time" (1 Peter 1:3-5 TEV).

We too can learn to keep our eyes on Jesus and on the joy set before. Particularly in the middle of difficult crises, but even in the round of our daily tasks, we can lose our perspective and become unnecessarily "fussed up" or disturbed or despairing. When we are tempted to give up on our own problems or the larger problems of nation and world, we can regain our perspective by looking to Jesus in faith and by keeping before us the joyful prospect of the peace that we shall have with him.

I rejoice as I keep my eyes on Jesus.

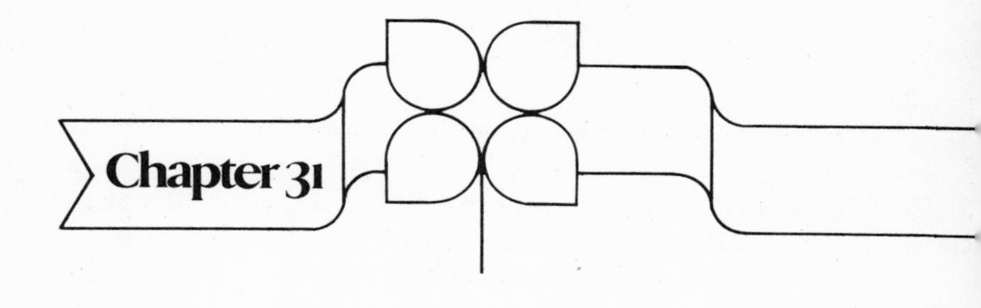

Everlasting Joy

Yours shall be everlasting joy.

Isaiah 61:7

We are living in a period of the most rapid change the world has ever seen. At least outwardly, life has changed more in the past 100 years than in the thousands of years preceding it. We have seen changes in transportation, communication, medicine, housing, clothing, family patterns, language, customs. There have been changes in the home, in the church, in the nation, in the world.

In such a welter and whirlwind of change, some have spoken of a new malady, future shock, caused by the inability to cope with such a rapid pace of change. The words of the hymn come to mind: "Change and decay in all around I see; O thou who changest not, abide with me."

Among the things that change here on earth is our joy. Many human joys fade. The joy of youthful strength and vitality wanes as our bodies slow down. The initial joy of a friendship or romance may wither. The joy of some new activity may pale into routine. Joy seems to be so fragile, so fleeting.

Yet Isaiah says, "Yours shall be *everlasting* joy." This everlasting joy begins in our life here on earth. But here it is always partial and changeable. God's promise is that the joy we experience here will one day be perfected, and then we will have everlasting joy which no one can take from us.

A character in Thornton Wilder's play *Our Town* says, "I don't care what they say with their mouths—everybody knows that something is eternal. And it ain't earth, and it ain't even stars . . . everybody knows in their bones that something is eternal, and that something has to do with human beings. All the greatest people ever lived have been telling us that for five thousand years and yet you'd be surprised how people are losing hold of it. There's something way down deep that's eternal about every human being."

Jesus said, "I go to prepare a place for you." He didn't tell us very much about this place. Perhaps since he has chosen to reveal so little, he doesn't want us to think about that eternal home too much. It is possible, as someone has said, to be so heavenly minded that we are no earthly good. But the Bible does give us some glimpses of our eternal life beyond death:

1. It will be a place of unsullied joy. The Bible uses all sorts of picture language to describe heaven, as if the writers were exhausting themselves in an attempt to express the inexpressible. They talk about streets of gold, about precious stones, about banquet feasts, about great white-robed choruses—all the images of joyful magnificence they can find. One of the most beautiful pictures is in the book of Revelation, the Christian's great song of triumph: "They shall hunger no more, neither thirst any more; the sun shall not strike them, nor any scorching heat. For the Lamb in the midst of the throne will be their shepherd, and he will guide them to springs of living water; and God will wipe away every tear from their eyes" (7:16-17).

2. *We shall be like him, for we shall see him as he is.* We will be transformed, so that we leave behind all our weaknesses and shortcomings. We will have a glorious body, like Christ's glorious body.

3. *Above all, we will be with God.* This will be the true source of all our joy. We can be with him now; we can know the joy of his presence now. But here, because of sin, that joy will always be incomplete. Here our joy begins, but here we have no abiding city; we seek one to come. That is the city of God where our joy will find eternal fullness. We will be with him, and that will be joy complete and perfect and eternal.

"Now to him who is able to keep you from falling and to present you without blemish before the presence of his glory with rejoicing, to the only God, our Savior through Jesus Christ our Lord, be glory, majesty, dominion, and authority, before all time and now and for ever. Amen" (Jude 1:25).

Everlasting joy is mine.